The Thrid
Book of Boobs

This book contains yet another selection
of the misprints and absurdities
culled from the press by Private Eye.

The majority were sent in by readers,
to whom our thanks are due

The court heard that West was seen driving erractically in Petersham Road, Richmond, on February 18th. She was stopped in Onslow Road, and taken to Richmond police station where a breast test proved positive.

Richmond & Twickenham Times

The Thrid Book of boobs from Private Eye

Illustrations by
Nick Newman

Private Eye

Published in Great Britain in September 1985 by
Private Eye Productions Ltd.
6 Carlisle Street, London W1,
in association with André Deutsch Ltd,
105 Great Russell Street, London WC1.

ISBN 0 233 97823 2

© Pressdram Ltd 1985

Designed by Roger Lightfoot

Private Eye acknowledges with thanks
the loan of a Selex 60AZ photocopier by
Selex (UK) Ltd, Croydon, Surrey,
to prepare the artwork for this book.

Printed and bound by
The Bath Press, Bath,

A DETERMINED campaign to halt the erosion of the ancient writ of babeas forpus is likely to reach the floor of the House of Commons early in the next ses-

The Observer

The Western Gazette

Cyclist butted car driver

A RAILWAY WORKER told York magistrates yesterday that he was in "a pretty high state emotionally" when he assaulted a motorist in Poppleton Road.

David William Morrill, aged 34, said he had had to swerve into the road when the motorist opened his car door as he cycled past.

He had been involved in pay negotiations that morning, and a bad period in pregnancy.

York Evening Press

Bodies needed to look after tombs

BUS BINGO

The Lincolnshire Road Car Co., which is losing £70,000 a month, may introduce "bus bingo" on its bus routes in South Humberside and Lincolnshire soon. Numbers would be displayed on the outside of buses and cards put through doors of horses in the area.

Daily Telegraph

Name rejected

A SUGGESTION that new homes on a site at New Moston, Manchester, should be called Poyser Bullock Walk after a former rector was turned down — councillors fear the name would be vandalised too often.

Manchester Evening News

During the month of May, Henekey's steak bar willbe supporting the Mayor's appeal for £45,000 towards an Emisonic Scanner for Windsor's King Edward VII Hospital.

For every customer who dies in the bar during the month, 20p will be donated towards the fund.

The Staines Informer

MR. D. D. DESAI
President, Gujarat Samaj

requests the pleasure of the company of

Mr. & Mrs. F. Chambers

to meet

THE WARSHIP THE MAYOR & MAYORESS CII. D. MALLAN

PEASANTS   £4.98 brace

Fresh Oven-ready
5 brace at £4.80 per brace
for the freezer
FARMER JACKS
137 Granton Road 65-67 East London Street 6 Whitehouse Loan

KP for Koster

NEW GROUP product manager at KP Foods is John Koster, previously with Kentucky Fried Children. Mr Koster joins the KP Nuts team and his responsibilities will include KP Disco's.

Super Marketing

Limbcentre hit by a walk-out

Cumberland News

£250.000 will

MR JAMES CROOKS, the thorat surgeion who operated on four embers of the Royal Family left estate valued at £248,914 gross, £247.499 net in his will published yesterday.

Liverpool Daily

LECTURES & MEETINGS

MANCHESTER INSTITUTE FOR THE DEATH. AGM at the Institute, Monday, October 1, 1979, 3 15 pm.

Grauniad

PRESIDENT Carter cancelled his appointments yesterday and was ordered to rest because of an " aggravated problem " with haemorrhoids. A White House spokesman said he was being treated by his personal physician, Rear Admiral William Lukash.—AP.

Grauniad

The royal couturier began his career as a small boy when he used his first box of paints to design a fancy dress costume for his cousin, who wore it to win first prize at a ball. School at Mill Hill and studies at Magdalene College, Cambridge, followed, but Sir Normun was not diverted from chiffon and hem.

He got the sack from his first job on Christmas Eve, 1922, and joined his sister in a dress

The Guardian

● BRIAN COUGH

Evening Times

★ **Words that Name Things.** Your child looks at the illustration, learns the key name or noun and dozens of related words and ideas.

★ **Words that Do Things.** From a simple word like 'burn', he learns a host of other verbs or doing words such as 'sizzle', 'smoke', and 'smoulder'.

New Zealand Listener

LONGFIELD SUITE, PRESTWICH
TEA DANCES
Every Wednesday, 1 30-4 pm, 40p.
Free Parking.
Tel 061-773 3769
**Apologies for last week's mix-up
(with the Vicars).**

Manchester Evening News

Hot Wind In Nepalgunj

Nepalgunj, April 11:

The streets here are deserted towards the afternoons because the growing heat has been worsened by loo, reports RSS.

Three persons who have taken ill in the loo are undergoing treatment at Bheri Zonal hospital.

Consumption of onions and cold things is said to be helpful in coping with the loo it is believed.

The Rising Nepal

A turkey is now a highly exonomical bird and can be burned into a number of interesting savoury dishes for the post Christmas period.

Oxford Star

4th PROFFESIONAL PERSON WANTED to share flat in Chelsea with 3 girls (female preferrable) hot and cold running men Please phone 352 - 9469.

Australian Give-away

Subs sale still rankles

CHINA has again demanded again that Dutch diplomatic relations with the Netherlands be downgraded

Straits Times

Viscount De L'Isle, V.D., K.G.,

MAN DIES ON CHAIR LIFT

Mr Angus McLeod, aged 62, of Bhuna Monadh, High Street, Kingussie, died yesterday on the chairlift about 2500 feet up on the Cairngorms.

Mr McLeod was on his way to help in running the Hillender ski race.

An Indonesian Navy frigate, Samadikun, has been sent to the area.

Dundee Evening Telegraph

The latest Public Authority Standard, just issued, is the first of a two-part set of guidance notes on the use of lubricating oils in the pubic sector.

Marketfact

55 new homes, including some sheltered homes for the elderly, are being built on this site. Access to the burial ground has been allowed for.

Putney Town Centre Plan

BERKSHIRE AND OXON

Meeting at the Thomas Hughes Hall, Uffington, Faringdon, on Tuesday, February 24, at 2pm. Mrs M Thatcher will talk on "The history of Arran". Arran-knitted clothes, fabric pictures and woodcraft made by Mrs Thatcher will be on sale.

Farmers Weekly

CENTRAL OTAGO STUD FARM
requires
SINGLE YOUNG MAN

Southland Times

Traffic tailed back as far as Hemel Hempstead from the contra-flow system near the Berry Grove junction at Bushey where a bride is being re-painted at night and during weekends.

Luton Evening Post-Echo

MRS THATCHER disclosed today she gets away from the pressures of politics by letting her hair down with women she can trust.

Halifax Evening Courier

At a resumed preliminary tribunal hearing in Birmingham yesterday Mrs Phyllis Robinson said that after he was sacked, Mr Robinson became difficult to live with. "He did strange things, like being deep in thought."

Daily Telegraph

Steel faced his colleagues with an ultimatum. Either they accepted the idea of a pact or they didn't

Grauniad

Douglas Bader pub

A new public house at Martlesham, near Ipswich, has been named after Sir Douglas Bader, the R A F's legless wartime hero.

Daily Telegraph

Sir Eric to stay

Sir Charles Villiers, 66, is to stay on as British Steel chairman for a year after his contract expires next September.

Portsmouth Evening News

MARGARET Trudeau, enstrangled wife of Canadian Prime Minister **Pierre Trudeau** is seen above covering her mouth with her hand as she confides in artist **Andy Warhol** in New York. She may have been telling Warhol that she's just signed a contract to star in the film *Kings and Desperate Men.*

Kenya Daily Nation

Sir James Goldsmith financier, businessman, and multi-millionaire will be talking to David Dimbleby in Person to Person on BBC 1, Thursday. (X29).

Papers in Iran headlined the deal, not as a compromise, but as a victory. "It's over. The Great Stan bows to all our demands," said the newspaper *Ka Han*, using the term used by Iranian officials to describe the United States.

Daily Telegraph

★St Martin's West St, Cambridge Circus, WC2 (836 1443). Leicester Square tube. 'The Mousecrap' by Agatha Christie. Of course Robert Mark put a stop to this sort of thing. . . . Mon-Sat 8.00, Tue 2.45, Sat 5.00 (Runs 2¼ hrs) £1.25, £2, £3, £4.

Time Out

An end to postal deliveries to individual flats in blocks was predicted by Sir William Barlow, the Post Office chairman yesterday.

Sir William told a House of Comons Select Coittee that he would like to see the new legislation due to go before Parliaent in the autun drop the legal requireent for individual deliveries to flats where there is a coon entrance.

The Times

Praise for new loo plan

By Diane Tonge

B A T H city Councillor Denis Lovelace was last praised for his efforts to reopen toilets on the city's Bog Island.

McMenemy was shattered. After locking his team away for a real talking to, he came out of the dressing room to say :

"It was our worst performance and our worst result.

"I blame myself. When you are 4-0 up, you should never lose 7-1.

Daily Express

PRINCESS ANNE presents the new colours to Flt. Lt. Andy Clarke.

The Wiltshire Times

MUSIC AS HELP IN DYSLEXIA

By John Izbicki, Education Correspondent

K^ING'S College Choir School, Cambridge, is to put to the test a theory that children who suffer from an ear, nose or throat infection in infancy are likely to experience difficulty in learning to read and become "word glind."

Daily Telegraph

MRS CHRISTINE OVERY, 32, of Golden Green, who was tied to a refrigerator door at gunpoint by two raiders, has been praised for her coolness by Tonbridge police.

Kent and Sussex Courier

EXPERIENCED SKIVERS

Two skivers are required in our footwear closing unit at Manor Road, Mancetter.

Advertisement in Nuneaton Evening Tribune

There are daily flights from Reykjavik and planned excursions around the virginity.

Guide to Reykjavik

Wanted Assistant To Travel Overseas

Investment Company Director requires assistant to travel overseas, preference given to Singapore; Malaysia and U.S.A. visa holder. Good remuneration, free tickets, food and broad. Please dial telephone number H-263551.

MR. TOBY JESSEL — 'loathsome'

Richmond & Twickenham Times

Staffordshire Area Health Authority
Mid-Staffordshire Health District
WHITE LODGE COMMUNITY UNIT

State Enrolled Nurse, SEN
(MENTALLY SUBNORMAL)

Express & Star, Wolverhampton

An 18-year-old Trent youth let more than his hair down after he had been drinking all day — he also dropped his trousers, twice.

The cheek of John Curley, 11 John Crescent was described in detail at East Lothian District Court on Tuesday.

East Lothian Courier

PALACE. S cc. 01-437 6834. From Sept. 17. The Fabulous New Production of

OKLAHOMO !

The Times

WIDOWER, aged 85, seeks company of widow, aged between 90 and 95, for social outings and friendship. Must be romantically inclined. Box A88.

Evening Express

In the United States four Libyan diplomats accused of intimidating Libyan dissidents are being recalled under an agreement reached between Washington and Tripoli.

It was reported yesterday that Scotland Yard strongly murdered two opponents of Colonel Qadhafi in London

The Observer

BECKMAN INSTRUMENTS LIMITED
QUEENSWAY, GLENROTHES, FIFE

require a

THICK FILM ENGINEER

South Wales Echo

Error in report

THERE was a typographical error in the report in last week's Gazette about List's bakery in Greenford.

The report, which read Mr List, who lies in Cervantes Court, Green Lane, Northwood, should have said Mr List, who lives in Cervantes Court, Green Lane, Northwood.

Greenford & Northholt Gazette

Hair by Stephen
Formerly Elizabeth

Hairdressing for ladies & gentlemen
Have your hair cut in the new Purdey style, now!

Newcastle & Tunstall Advertiser

R. BODDY
FUNERAL SERVICE
365, HOLDERNESS ROAD

New Private Chapel of Repose.

Day and Night Service

Tel. 29327.   mtc

Hull Daily Mail

The prize was Vernon's top dividend for last week and was won for a weekly payment of £12.65. "My wife always posed tit for us," said Mr Durling. "Now I think she deserves a damn good holiday while the pub is being cleaned up.

The Mercury

ENTREES

Oja au Merguez (Scrambled Eggs With Sausages	1.800
Plain Omelette	1.300
Choice of omelette (*cheese or ham or fine herbes*)	1.700
Brick with Egg and Tunafish	1.500

Tunis hotel menu

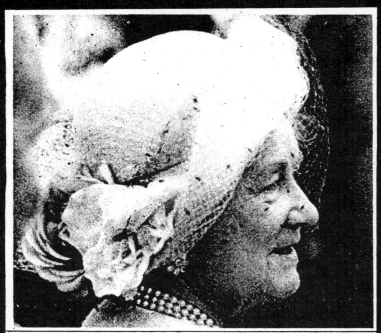

"Adopt a granny" is social service idea

Sale & Altrincham Messenger

MR. ANTHONY BLUNT

Mr. Maxwell-Hyslop asked the Prime Minister whether Mr. Anthony Blunt is in receipt of any person from public funds, in respect of his public services.

The Prime Minister : No.

Hansard

Widow Mrs. Eva Dednam, 80, was "very comfortable" in West Suffolk Hospital last night after being pulled from a pond near her home at Newton Green, near Sudbury.

Mrs. Dednam, of Plampins Close, was found floating semi-conscious in the pond at the village green on Saturday.

Local resident Mr. Bill Duckling discovered her in two feet of water.

East Anglian Daily

MR. LAI KUAN LIAN
DEPARTED: 5TH JAN. 1979

GONE BUT NOT FORGOTTEN. LIKE WINE, HIS MEMORY WILL NEVER BE DULLED BY THE PASSAGE OF LIME AND WILL ALWAYS BE CHERISHED IN THE HEARTS OF FAMILY, FRIENDS, AND ALL WHO KNEW HIM.

Straits Settlement Times

SPITALFIELDS NEIGHBOURHOOD LAW SERVICE
seeks

A Community Lawyer
Two Housing Rights Workers

The Law Service covers the ward of Spitalfields, a depraved inner-city area with

Law Society Gazette

FIVE well-bred Ferrets, only reason for sale, owners leg injuries. — Tel. Weston-super-Mare

Western Daily Press

David Barber, 28, of Norfolk Crescent, Bath, was already on bail after being arrested while trying to smuggle morphine through London Airport from India, said Mr David Morris, prosecuting. He was jailed for six years after admitting evading drug import regulations, burglary and reckless diving.

Daily Telegraph

Barnwell said : 'If I have a future in football then it will denitely — and I mean denitely — be with Wolves.

Daily Mail

GOOD PRICE FOR ATLAS

A large atlas in two volumes dating from 1844 made £290 at a book auction conducted by Thomas Watson and Son in Darlington recently. Other main prices were: 18th cent political magazines £52; Mr Sponge's Sporting Tour, R S Surtees, £42; The Holy Bible, Geneva version, 16th cent, £21; Survey of The High Roads from London, John Cary, £130; two post-card albums containing 100 cards each, £34; First edition winner the Poof, A A Milne, £57; An

Darlington & Stockton Times

The examiners appointed by the Board of the Faculty of English Language and Literature give notice that A. J. HOLLINGHURST, Magdalen College, having submitted a thesis on 'The creative uses of homosexuality in E. M. Forster, Ronald Firbank, and L. P. Hartley', will be orally examined on Monday, 3 December, at 2.30 p.m. in the St. Cross Building.

S. DE. R. WALL
P. N. FURBANK
Examiners

FIRE STATION
It will be much easier to find the Fire station in future as on Wednesday last a sign reading "Fire Station" was erected outside the Station.

American research, which is gaining support in Britain, shows that problem drinkers have recognisable habits, gulping or taking large sips of their drinks, and rarely putting their lasses down.

Grauniad

Schizophrenic

killed

herself

with two

plastic bags

Milton Keynes Gazette

A L i v e r p o o l shipping office manager turned to fraud after l e a d i n g a "blameless life", London Bankruptcy Court was told on Wednesday.

Thomas Gilbert Swindells, 54, whose home is at 22 Links View, Wallasey, was said to have debts of £108,100 and assets of

Wallasey News

MALE 22, seek screwing position, long cruise. Some experience. Mike Brown 0273 733656.
M123

Yachting Monthly

The young lawyer told his OAU audience:

"The body of the imperialist octopus may be sitting in South Africa, Namibia, Zimbabwe, Mozambique, Angola and Guinea-Bissau, but its testacles are stretching over our entire continent."

I noticed that he was cheered from all corners of the conference hall. Note his strong- to-the-point African language in denouncing imperialism.
Kenya

REPRESENTATIVES from the Theatre Authority flew to Aswan yesterday to supervise the final preparations for the celebrations to take place on the 10th of this month, on the re-opening of the temples of Philae on Agilka island.

A new symphony, by the Czechoslovakian composer Devur Jack, will be played by the Orchestra. The symphony, is called «The New World».

The Egyptian Gazette

After an insurance policy matured, the family went to London and he bought the drug in a public house. The next day, police searched his home.

The bench ordered the drug confiscated, but allowed Aggatt to keep the pot.

The Western Morning News

Mr Morris said catalogue of injuries inflicted on public transport staff was horrifying including bloody noses, fractured paws and broken arms and legs. He wanted magistrates to take a tougher view of such assaults.

One delegate from Gloucestershire called for the return of the "cat" to punish offenders, but Mr Morris said that was not the answer.

New Standard

SECRETARY

A varied position where you can really get stuck director you will enjoy in. As secretary to a stimulation as you are trained into various as pects of this interesting position.

The Sunday Tribune (Durban)

Homosexual law reform approved

By JAMES NAUGHTIE,

The Scotsman

Oxford City Council is to press the Thames Water Authority to help improve sanity facilities along the river banks running through the city.

Oxford Times

Australia's Prime Minister, Mr Malcolm Fraser, yesterday announced seeping measures to conserve the use of fuel. The aim is to cut consumption of petrol by 10 per cent by increasing the price of fuel for motorists.

Guardian

JEWISH BLIND SOCIETY

The present Executive Director is due to retire early in 1981, and applications are invited for the position of

DEPUTY DIRECTOR

with a view to succeeding as Executive Director. This is a challenging position in Jewish social work and requires a person with ability, tact and vision.

Observer

In order to better the service and the welcome given to tourists that visit Spain, the Secretariat of State for Tourism is undertaking a publicity campaign, which, with the slogan "Tourism benefits everyone, take care of tit", hopes to increase the attention and affability given to the tourist not only by the professionals who work in this sector but also by the public in general.

Spanish Tourist Office information

"Then the horse got up but Mark Phillips just lay on the ground.

"At this point a Mrs Ayres who was nearest to him, rushed over. She thought he might have been dead, but as she got near to him he started to get up.

"He was dazed and groggy and told her: 'It's not my legs, it's not my ars, it's my hand.'"

Western Daily Press

HEARSE

1975 GRANADA GHIA FOR SALE
New Duffy body.   Ph. 0503-31586

Irish Independent

in November   1971. The
islands, Abu Musa and the
Great and Little Tumbs, are
vital to control the Strait
of Hormuz, through which
two tankers an hour ferry
cruds to the west,

Rising Nepal

...way Corporation was presented.
   After reaching, the Hong Kong side,
Princess Alexandra unveiled a plague
commemorating the completion of the
system. A community

The Hong Kong Trader

WILDEBEESTS-LEGGES (MABEL). —
Died October 2, 1979, and good
riddance too I say

The Grauniad

The idea is for her to participate in the "Adventurous Women" session, which will also include talks by such celebrated adventurers as Carolyn Oxton, who has explored the Zaire River, and Araina Stassinopoulus, who has appeared on the BBC.

Campaign

'GROW OWN FOOD' CAMPAIGN

Mr GREGORY JOHNSON, West Devon, moving, said we must not offer the French the opportunity to flood our market with their paralysed milk and inferior apples. We must buy British.

The Daily Telegraph

DUREX PROTECTIVES. Price list and "Marriages are Mad" booklet sent post free without obligation. Marital Aid Catalogue added upon request. H. Fiertag (Dept. S.) 34 Wardour St. W.1.

Spectator

Alice takes a fine picture, and she's a good photographer too. She combines these attributes with a keen business acumen that's the envy of the Institute.

CENTRE

Hunting the stag was the traditional occupation at Lyme and the origin of the house. It still has a herd of Deer. The park at Lyme runs to thirteen hundred acres and rises to 850 feet on a Cheshire spur of the Pennines. It used also to be famous for Lyme mastiffs, exceptionally large breasts, some of them the size of a small pony.

British Rail leaflet

Mr Bath —
Miss Tubb

THE WEDDING took place at St Paul's Chu.ch, Ru hall, of Miss Sally Elizabeth Tubb, only daughter of Mr and Mrs K. J. Tubb of 17 Allan Close, Rusthall, and Mr Benjamin James Bath, youngest son of Mrs R. Bath of 19 Allan Close and the late Mr J. Bath.

Kent & Sussex Courier

Enkalon is to get £1,500,000 via the Northern Ireland Office to keep the textiles and carpet yarn factory open for another seven moths

Daily Telegraph

BOY WANTED TO KILL THE QUEEN
Centre Pages

Daily Mail

QUEEN MOTHER HAS ULSTER ON LEG

P.A. news tape

INTERIORS LTD.
KING & MARKET STREET   PHONE 21631
OPEN MON-SATURDAY 9-5 P.M.

JUST ARRIVED

Large Shipment
of

WICKER FURNITURE

IT WON'T. LAST LONG !!

OPEN 9-5 p.m.
MONDAY TO SATURDAY

Nassau Grauniad

Godfrey had further talks with striker Peter Rogers yesterday and Rogers has now finally agreed to sing a new contract.

Dave Pullar has still not settled on new terms, but the fact that he has taken so long to see Godfrey about his contract is seen as a good sign.

There are not supposed to be any problemshhh

Exeter Express and Echo

Exposed himself

HIGH WYCOMBE police are looking for a man who indecently exposed himself to a woman on the bridge in Cock Lane on Monday night.

Bucks Free Press

Patrons please note that the 'Daily Times' of Wednesday 4th June published the name of the actor for the film **Deadly Harvest** as **Cunt Walker** by error, but it should have read **Clink Walker**. We regret the inconvenience caused.

Daily Times (Malawi)

Required by Dublin based market research company

School lever
Male/Femaly

Southside (Dublin)

CHARTERED ACCOUNTANT

The Scotsman

Testament begins as the diary of a provincial young lady, deceptively pretty-pretty with more brians and passion than seemed altogether proper at the time. *Grauniad*

chairman of the jury, of Humphrey Burton, who recently stepped down as head of B B C music and arts programmes. For the B C has never yet succeeded in winning a Prix Italia in this category—though it has a bugger output of serious music than I TV.

Daily Telegraph

Correction

We would like to offer our apologies to J. B. Reynier Ltd. for a caption error that appeared in a recent issue. The picture published was not, of course, of Miss Carolyn Reynier —It was in fact a broken-down egrappoir.

Harpers & Queen

Moving Mr Donlon may also have a domestic political benefit for Mr Haughey. Some of his backbenchers are worried by the threat to their future posed by Mr Blaney's pianos

Grauniad

Gays walk tall

THE BIGGEST gay celebration ever seen outside the USA takes place in Britain next week: Gay Pride Wee 1979.

New Musical Express

HARROW WEST CONSERVATIVE ASSOCIATION PINNER WARD

SURGERY

Cllr. Mrs. Marjorie Crick
Cllr. Mrs. Jill Clack
and
Cllr. Owen Cock

will be available to Constituents on

Harrow Observer

special presentation was made to Sam Bartram, who kept goal for Charlton in more than 800 matches, including wart-time appearances.

David Lacey

Grauniad

"Up to this day they still do not know that I sat perched on top of the ladder and had a front-row seat," he said.

The most satisfying play which Mr Brooke staged was the musical Irma La Douche, while his "biggest flop was a musical which I had written — it only lasted 10 days".

Islington Gazette

In a varied early career he helped to run a dance hall in South London, became a Red Coat at Butlins and worked for the Berni Inns group, rising to become a manager at one low point in his life.

Sunday Express

Mr Oxford said: "I have no doubt at all that this is not a racial issue, as such. It is exclusively a crowd of black hooligans intent on making life unbearable and indulging in criminal activities."

The Grauniad

Michael Malenki, 38, of Koikin village in East Sepik Province was fined K40 for assaulting Fr Dambui and K60 for being unlawfully on the Premier last Wednesday.

Papua New Guinea Post Courier

STRADIVARI OF Tomorrow. Violins and cellos for soloists made by finest living Italian masters who have extinguish themselves at most important international competition. Exclusively at Rocksom Piano Co. Ltd., 244 Hennessy Rd., H.K. 5-740286 Mr. Chu.

South China Morning Post

His lawyer William Dunn added; "I am grateful to the Record for their help.

"I have been trying for some time to get my client into prison."

Daily Record

Police at hawick yesterday called off a search for a 20-year-old man who is believed to have frowned after falling into the swollen River Teviot.

The Scotsman

Cricket season opens in style

Times of Zambia

8.30 World in Action.
9.0 Quincy — a Japanese marital art superstar dies, but Japanee customs prohibit an autopsy.

The Express & Echo

FIT. RELIABLE trustworthy, adaptable 41-yr.-old rusty messenger seeks work in City. Immediate start, 804

Evening Standard

What Mrs Thatcher's closest friends are wondering is whether, as the signs suggest, she is beginning to suffer from metal fatigue.

Grauniad

WASHINGTON, Oct. 1 — Japan's new Minister of Finance, Michio Watanabe, warned of stagnant world trade and even disorder in world finance if countries pile up huge international deficits or fail to get back the money that countries with surpluses are accumulating.

"We can not dispel the pear," he said.

Hong Kong Standard

THE driver stopped a late-night bus after James Emerson started fighting with a woman passenger, it was said at Salford magistrates court last Thursday.

21-year-old Emerson then began arguing with police who were called to the bus on Eccles New Road at 2 a.m. on April 25.

"He was in a very drunken policeman's trouser leg during home," said Mr. Ken Smith, prosecuting.

Salford City Reporter

Palace security breached again

The discovery of another intruder in the grounds of Buckingham Palace has led to a further review of security there. A man who was discovered by a policeman from the Royal Protection Group said he was looking for Princess Anne. He was taken to a mental hospital

The Times

Mr. Paisley earlier criticised Buckingham Palace for inviting Cardinal Basil Hume to the wedding, saying it was "shameful" that the English Catholic Primate should be there.

This is believed to be a primary reason for St. Paisley's reluctance to say if he will be at St. Paul's.

Yorkshire Post

Lord Beeching, now 68 and retired, is still convinced he did the right thing in his railway organisation, but adds "Of course I don't like being remembered as the mad axeman; I just wasn't mad like that".

Stockport Advertiser

Mr Charles Vaggers, once Mr Thorpe's staunchest political ally and his local chairman until last March, said : "There is relief and euphoria today, and the red carpet will be rolled out if Mr Thorpe comes to Barnstaple. But questions remain in people's minds. A lot of queer things have been happening."

Sunday Express 24.6.79

Bent & Company

W. Roiter, LL.B.   J. Zucker, LL.B.

Solicitors

When the vote was called for on a show of hands Mr Newcombe announced: "That looks pretty unanimous for strike action." His words were drowned by a roar of protest. There were repeated shouts of "rubbish" and "it's a fox".

The Times

Dorset Evening Echo

MR GEOFFREY DICKENS, the MP whose hearing of the diplomat in the child-sex trial cover-up affair, with Mrs Maureen Knight, 43, who runs a Tunbridge Wells Nursing Home, for whom he has left his wife

Kent & Sussex Courier

Construction News

The best parts of the book are Clare Francis' personal descriptions of her "sex voyages of discovery", her experiences aboard the replica "Golden Hinde", her trip to the ocean bed in the submersible "Alvin" and her other visits.

Lloyd's List

MARRIED at the United Reformed Church, Exeter, were Miss Lesley Jayne Hamblin, daughter of Mr and Mrs B. Hamblin, of 20 Rowland Rise, Puriton, Somerset, and Mr Christopher Brian Parker, son of Mr and Mrs E. Parker, of 7 Dansborough Road, Bridgwater.

Bridesmaids were Miss Sara Jessop and Miss Christine Hallett. The best was was Mr Tony Ward.

Exeter Express & Echo

L'Abattoir

RESTAURANT

French, Italian and Greek Cuisine.

● FULLY LICENSED   ● SEATING FOR 60

196 High Street, Barnet

Barnet Press Group

PERSONAL

New Zealand: Male. Continental. 41, would like to hear from genuine female aged 25-35. Own teeth an advantage. Will be visiting Fiji April-May.
Please write to Mr P. Stattmann, G.P.O. Box 1893, Auckland, NZ.   '18.1

Fiji Times

President's 'chopper' was most popular

Morning Advertiser

SDP party — mass rally.

Kingston and Surrey Guardian

10.45
Morning Story
The Bum
by W. SOMERSET MAUGHAM
Read by John Westbrook
Producer MITCH RAPER

Radio Times

BLOOD AND VOMIT PROOF CARPET that looks like Wilton. Almost impossible to stain, put anywhere. 60 cols. £3.99 + vat. Samples 30p stamps Ollerton Hall DP, Knutsford, Cheshire.

Dental Practice

THE ELUSIVE GREAT BASTARD
The Hungarian project to ensure survival of the Great Bastard the largest bird in Europe　　11, 12

Radio Budapest broadcasts

GLASGOW

In our issue of November 30 we reported that the Lubavitch Foundation in Glasgow held a "dinner and ball" to celebrate its tenth anniversary. This was incorrect. A spokesman explained: "The Lubavitch movement does not have balls."

Jewish Chronicle

Provisional Sinn Fein said Mrs McCabe had been murdered by the police. A 16-year-old youth was shot dead by troops in West Belfast during disturbances on Wednesday. He was with other masked men in a vehicle carrying crates of petrol tombs.

Daily Telegraph

Middlesex Polytechnic

MA in Deviancy

Time Out

Amsterdam not suitable as London airport, says BAA

BY LYNTON McLAIN

BRACHI.—On May 8, to JACQUIE (née Kinnear) and ROBIN, a daughter (Kathryn Julienne Maryse), a sister for Anthony to poke.

Daily Telegraph

U.K. INTER-PROFESSIONAL GROUP

(This is the report referred to in Council News on page 462)

On the initiative of Sir David Napley, Past-President of the Law Society, a group of professional bodies, listed below, have made an informal arrangement for representatives to meet from time to time

The Journal of the Chartered Institute of Patent Agents

A DISTINGUISHED Colchester musician who translated operas while he was locked in railway lavatories for privacy as he commuted to London, has died, aged 72.

Mr Tom Hammond, formerly of Mile End, who also wrote an opera himself, became known to train conductors who, it was said, would call out: "Is that you Tom?" to which he would reply: "Yes. I'm just getting through act two."

Essex County Standard

GROCER FEARED BEING CABBAGE

North Devon Journal/Herald

There was determined support also from the injured Imran Khan, who helped Miandad add 61 for the sixth wicet. Miandad, who batted 139 minutes and hit seven fours, looked thoroughly capable of breaking India's strong grip.

When Imran left him, sixth out, Pakistan were almost halfway to their objective. Miandad was eighth to go. He was stretched well forward in defence when Doshi raped him on the pad, and successfully appealed for l b w to the umpire.

Daily Telegraph

Yard officers jailed for blackmail

Three officers of the Metropolitan Police were jailed at the Central Criminal Court last night for blackmailing and plotting corruptly to obtain Soraya Khashoggi.

The Times

The Conservative "Bum Group," in a recent pamphlet, has urged BL to seek a joint venture with Japan. Moves to import Japanese technology through joint ventures are already afoot in the television industry. In the glamorous

Christian Science Monitor

A vote for member unions to "unite and resist by all the beans within their power" Conservative economic policies, would have been seen by Ministers as a political advantage in the short term, reinforcing voters' desire for curbs on union activities.

Daily Telegraph

Even the one pig which was produced. a four-month-old called Jigs. was carried by its owner, Mr Michael Jones, rather than being let loose outside the Fairmont Hotel on Nob Hill where the Princess is stying.

Daily Telegraph

1.00 Pebble Mill at One: Studio interviews with Canadian film director Norman Jewison (Fiddler on the Roof, Thomas Crown Affair) and with ex-war artist Terence Cuneo, who has also pained royalty.

The Times

THE MEDICAL RESEARCH Fund, a recognised charity (Reg. 500359). has many vital research projects to maintain in the fight against disease. Help us to maintain this work and assist handicapped children. victims of cancer. heart disease and Lord Harlech. Medical Research Fund. 9 Kensington High St., London W8 5NP.

Sunday Times

Witnesses who saw three men walking into the corpse on Tuesday, and who saw two men run out after the shots, said the men were carrying long-barrelled weapons and a large ammunition magazine.

Daily Telegraph

SURREY
Education Committee
PORTLEY HOUSE SCHOOL
Whyteleafe Road, Caterham
Qualified TEACHER of the
Dead require at this school

When he descends to meet
the people, a certain diffi-
dence takes over. He finds
it difficult to approach people
and to say anything much
when he does. 'How do you
do? Roy Jenkins. Where do
you live?' are the usual
openers, perhaps followed by
an inquiry about possible
port.

The Observer

REDUNDANCY notices have
been issued after the shock
decision to axe another
Godalming factory.
Phoenix Omnitubes, the
flexible tube factory on the
Wharf will fold in September.

Surrey Advertiser

Bible in hand

Due to an error in trans-
mission we stated in an
inquest on Saturday that
Mrs Susanah Vincent, of
Porth, was found dead
with a bottle in her left
hand and a plastic bag
over her head. This should
have read "a bible in her
left hand." We apologise
for any distress caused to
the family.

*Swindon Evening
Advertiser*

**CHEAPEST SHAG
IN LEEDS**
**FOAMBACKED
4 FANTASTIC COLOURS**

Leeds Evening Post

Expert on Ugandan affairs to give Reith lectures

Broadcast

Why not come to THE CROWN at ALDBOURNE and have a meal - LUNCH or DINNER - in our private Dining Room or, for smaller parties, in the comfort of our open log fire.

But no wonder the green-fly came in their swarms (as did the audience) to hear such playing from the Royal Philharmonic Orchestra. Their technique was hot, the acoustic was dry — perfect breeding ground for green-fly as well as for the audience in the big marquee for the opening prom of the Folk Festival.

Cambridgeshire Evening News

A rates bombshell revealed by Chancellor Sir Geoffrey Howe in his mini-budget last week will hit domestic ratepayers in Gwynedd hard from next April.

Sir Geoffrey announced that the Government's bugger for rates, the

North Wales Chronicle

Last time out the Armagh boys accounted for Castle-blayney and the wide open spaces of Omagh will suit their style of play. It promises toben aeentr   fuck it — to be an entertaining game, which could go either way.

Irish News

LIGHT SNACKS

Slice Pork Pie ·80
Plough Person's Lunch ·85

The Reserve Bank, which manages the rand' sexchange rate, has apparently decided to call a halt to its slide.

Dr Gerhard de Kock, the bank's governor, said recently that the authorities were deter-mined to maintain the rand's external and internal value.

Financial Times

Sir,—I was saddened to read (Guardian, January 7) that Ilie Nastase was fined £2,500 for his recent antics at the doubles championships.

Rather than being fined, he should be paid the same amount for livening up what is otherwise a dreary game with long periods of waiting whilst self-important players moodily examine their balls. *Grauniad*

HAVE YOU SEEN THESE MEN?

MAN 1   MAN 2

Hartleypool Mail

☐ AN EASTERN MORNING. . . . .
A glass of fruit juice
Foul Madammes
Black Olives and labneh cheese served with Arabic bread

RUMANIA, faced with a birth rate which is so low that the population is steadily dwindling, is urging all women to have at least four chldren as their "patriotic duty."

Anyone found to be pregnant who fails to have a child faces awkward questions, and possible imprisonment, fines dismissal or demolition.

Daily Express

● THINK PRIDE. The new Bridgend operation has a notice at the door saying "Welcome to the best pruners and shears factory in the world." Using techniques such as these, the firm hopes to engender some of the pride in the workplace and the product which is second nature in many Japanese firms.

"Being blunt, we're not the best yet," Jim Harrower says.

Sunday Times

I, **SANDRA SHORT**, hereby give notice that I have, as from February 25, 1982, renounced my former name and have as from February 25, 1982, assumed the name of Sandra Long.

Grauniad

BY AN unfortunate typographical error in Prisea Middlemiss's article last Wednesday, Professor Ian Macgillivray and two of his colleagues were described as " abortion obstetricians " instead of " Aberdeen obstetricians." We apologise to the doctors concerned.

Grauniad

Nigel Lawson divorced

THE Financial Secretary to the Treasury, Mr Nigel Lawson, was divorced today because of his adultery with Therese Maclear a former consumer affairs specialist in the House of Commons library.

Evening Standard

Customs officials in Brest are interrogating 14 British divers who were allegedly caught with more than a ton of antique treasurers found in a ship sunk off the Brittany coast.

The Times

The director-general of the BBC, Mr Alasdair Milne, is expected to hold a further infiltration of the Conservative chief whip, Mr John Wakeham, this week.

Grauniad

Pumpkin problem

Todd Frakes, 2½, has a problem finding just the right pumpkin for his Halloween, jack-o'lantern, after more than five-inches of snow covered the pumpkins at a local fruit and vegetable stand. Todd is the son of Mr. and Mrs. Lonnie Frakes.

China Post

BEES BILL

[The LORD AIREDALE in the Chair].

Clause 1 (*Control of pests and diseases affecting bees*):

Lord HIVES moved Amendment No. 1.

Hansard

Abattoir staff will be halved

Chester Mail

A six-seat Victorian walnut loo table
in impeccable condition (£925).

Kent Life

The march will proceed from
St. Stephen's Green to Sim-
monscourt Road and a small
delegation will be deceived at
the British Embassy

Irish Press

MALE (24) seeks doom in central
flat. Please phone 031-44
6437.

Edinburgh Evening News

Mrs. Laxmibai, better known as Mai Bhide, all over Maharashtra, for her popular holes on the Marathi stage and in films died in a Bombay hospital today after a protracted illness. She was 61 and is survived by three sons.

Bombay Times

A9   Thanks
MIKE Heather and Julia wish to apologise for their behaviour when they got pissed on Wednesday 18th.

Standard (Nairobi)

Piped TV

I would like to point out that what I did in fact write was that the council forced piped TV "on us" not "up us" as printed in the County Times and Express on October 25.
T. A. WILKINSON,
14 Dolerw, Welshpool.

County Times & Express & Gazette

Law takes grip on sex industry

Pressure is building up against Soho sex establishments to introduce licences to control their growth and to help protect other traders.

This week the Greater London Council approved tentative legislation to make it illegal for sex shops to operate without licences.

The proposed legislation was instigated by Westminster City Council and is expected to come before Parliament in the New Year in the GLC's General Powers Bill.

Westminster has opposed the setting up of new sex establishments in Soho on planning grounds where possible, which has led to a flood of appeals.

The Department of the Environment has set aside three weeks in March and April next year to hear the 28 appeals, though the council's planning committee is currently considering 100 such cases. Chairman of the committee is Thomas Whipham.

Thomas Cook's North West regional manager since January 1967, died in his sleep during the company's branch managers conference in Palma, Majorca, last week.

Travel Trade Gazette.

A NORFOLK vicar has branded crematorium chapels "artificial" and "no place for any self-respecting member of the church to go to."

"I would not be seen dead in one," said the Rev. David Roland-Shrubb.

Eastern Evening News

But according to the report published by the Welsh Office, school rules can work only if they are accepted separately by pupils and staff alike. And schoolgirls forced to wear burgundy coloured knockers are accusing the school of being petty.

Rhondda Leader

"From the very beginning Mr. Flynn has observed his pledge of confidentiality to the source by taking precautions to conceal even from his closet colleagues any information which could indicate the identity of the source."

Financial Times

On Tuesday evening there was a "Pub Night" to introduce new members of the Commonwealth Association at the social center in Altamira. It was enthusiastically attended by Their Excellencies, **Matthew** and **Morfydd William**, Ambassador from Grenada and recently arrived here; **Peter** and **Myrian Mayling**; **Misty Wilkinson**, who has recently returned from a year in England; **Norman Brisbane** and his daughter, **Molly**, from Canada (Norman, I understand plays the "bagpipes"); **Brian** and **Sheila Gordon, Alex Sanderson** who has recently arrived to join his parents here, **Ann** and **Tom Langford** and their daughter, **Debbie**, a charming girl who is visiting from England; **Rosalind Masson; John Watkins; Irmgard** and **Barry Walker, George** and **Everild Edmunds**. I believe it was almost enjoyable. ——O——

The Daily Journal (Venezuela)

Saturday, June 19, was a hectic day for the wood rolling fraternity on Ammanford bawling green.

Carmarthen Journal

The Loc Nar, a glowing green ball, then goes on to menace his daughter by relating a series of inconsequential tales in which its evil has featured. She backs away horrified, as well she might, listening to the Tories

Film and Television Technician

Apt. 401, Aust. Embassy Staff Apts., 11-39, Mita 1-chome, Minato-ku.

Group Captain R.J. BOMBALL,

Defence and Air Force Attaché.

(8. 12. 78)   Mrs. Bomball (Aileen)
Miss Bomball (Susan)

Tokyo Diplomatic List

The Left-wing Labour Co-ordinating Committee yesterday launched a new attck onm the party leadership, demanding an end to "withch-hunts and hit lists" and calling on front bench spokesmen to end their "preoccupation" with interanal manoeuvrings.

Lloyd's List

GREAT HELP TO MALTA

Former Governor recalls siege

Lt.-Gen. Sir William G. Dobbie, who was Governor of Malta from 1940-42 and is famous for his fart in the defence of the island,

8.05 **REPUTATIONS:** Kenneth Tynan (1927-80) Her career reassessed

0.05 STUART BURROWS SINGS

Durham and Chester-Le-Street Trader

An article (The Star, November 7) says Mrs Marietjie Viljoen, wife of South Africa's State President, would like to have R200 000 collected on "Our Children's Day" and a fund-raising campaign.

I have another idea to collect funds for this purpose. The Argus Printing and Publishing Company should agree to give one cent for every misprint in The Star during November 1981. It would come to quite a lot, although I don't believe it would reduce the number of misprints.

Misprints

Berea.

★ *November is a heavy publishing month for all newspapers and with large issues misprints inevitably increase. Note, however, that there are 5 000 characters in every full column of type. Even if there are five misprints a column that is only an error of 0,1 percent. We are working constantly on the problem, aiming to keep problem, aiming to keep — Editor.*

The Star, Johannesburg.

FORMER Labour Cabinet Minister Lord George-Brown is to appear before Hailsham Magistrates on a drink-drive charge.

Lord George-Brown, 67, of Willingdon Lane, Jevington, has been summoned to appear on January 12.

His name appeared by mistake on the list of cases due to be heard by the court on Tuesday.

Representing Lord George-Brown, Mr Christopher Stredder said there had been an "unfortunate hiccup" which was not the fault of his client.

Sussex Express

If the founder of the Press, who usually thought in terms of centuries rather than years, were alive, he would turn in his grave.

Sunday Tribune (Dublin)

Grauniad

PIANO for sale. Good condition, price £40. Delivery M.o.T. included — Phone after 9pm 6. 3543.

Nottingham Evening Post

Oman imported 6,015 tonnes of general cargo from Japan in the month of July, followed by Singapore (4,959 tonnes) and Taiwan (4,604 tonnes) in the month. of July.

Automobile dealers imported 5,268 vehicles from Japan followed by West Germany (602 vehicles) and the United States (555 vehicles in the same period.

Alfred Brendel plays Beethoven's "Appassionata".

Times of Oman

Also staying on the first floor was Mr Nigel Lawson, the Chancellor. Those staying on the second floor included Mr John Gummer, party chairman, and Lord Gowrie, the wets minister.

Graniaud

With the Chief Constable will be Division Commander Chief Supt. Peter Skinner, and Chief Inspector G. Bollard, of the traffic division.

Buckingham Advertiser

USHERS **THE TELEGRAPH** USHERS

58 BRIDGE STREET, TAUNTON, SOMERSET.

VARIED MEN AT SENSIBLE PRICES
FINE BEERS

Somerset County Gazette

"To the best of our knowledge and belief we have complied with the general conditions of the Fair Wages Resolution passed by the House of Commons on 14th October, 1946 for at least three months preceding the date of this application for inclusion on the Standing Lists".

Contractors failing to submit the above information or/and declaration will normally be executed.

City of Bristol City Engineer's Department advertisement

Bargain Corner Items Under £15

TRAVELCOT, £12. Playpen, £10. Highchair, £8. Breeding cage, £8. — 69339.

Leicester Mercury

Douglas Lowe, from England, to his sister, Frances Matcheson, of San Bernardino, Mr Lowe suffered a fatal blood clot in a lung and Mrs Matcheson died of police, it said.

Grauniad

GRANADA As London except: 1.20pm Granada Reports. **1.30** Take the high road. **2.00** Television superbowel. **3.45** News. **3.30-**

The Times

Mr Roberto Frassetto, one of the experts, said yesterday that the first mobile dame, which will be laid across the Lido entrance to the lagoon, could be completed "in five weeks time"

Grauniad

HOW dare Ian Craig report that the Conservative party conference was inspired by Dave Eager's "daft speech."

(Mrs) M E Booth, Clayton.

FOOTNOTE: Sorry. A technical fault. It should have read "deft" instead of "daft."

Manchester Evening News

He told the House that expansion of the Tanga Steel Rolling Mill will be completed this year to enable it produce 40,000 tonnes of steel annually using local materials.

He explained that metal working and engineering industries produced less goods last year compared to 1981 because they still depended wholly on imported raw materials. The affected items included oxen-drawn razor blades and radios, he added.

Sunday News, Tanzania

57, tells me: 'It's the first time in 10 years that we've been let down in this way. Melting the Princess's family would have been the highlight of the week, but there you are.'

Daily Mail Diary

Glider crash

ASPATRIA: Hang glider Gordon Rigg ended up in hospital this week with an arm injury after crashing during a flight from Great Cockup Fell, Skiddaw.

Cumberland News

Hardy Amies.

Hardy Amies, likes a good light read by Victoria Holt or Jean Plaidy where she can see herself in the leading role,

London Portrait Magazine

Pride of Canada

Among 115 things which readers of the Canadian magazine Today chose as reasons to be proud of their country were the Mounties, the scenery, Pierre Trudeau, an Ontario hospital for sick owls, and the loon's mating call.

Financial Times

Cars stationary

Two car drivers involved in an accident in Newion Road, Torquay, reported in Wednesday's Herald Express, ask us to make clear that their vehicles were in fact stationary at the time and that neither skidded.

LOST, brown and black dog, has pie-balled left eye and limps, got half of right ear missing and no tail, answers to the name of Lucky. — Finder please call at Land-Rover Centre.

Huddersfield Examiner

Wednesday, 31st October at 2.00 p.m.

Dr. N. Rock (British Geological Survey, Edinburgh)

"The Geology of Sumatra"

University of Ashton, Dept. of Geological Sciences

Dear Guest,

On September 30, 1984 winter timing will start. As of 12:00 midnight all clocks will be forward one hour back.

Truly yours,

The Management

Hotel Marriott, Cairo

BREDA Finn and Steven Day were married at St Joseph's Church, Epsom.

The bride is the daughter of Mr and Mrs J. Finn, of Melton Place, Epsom. The groom is the son of Mr and Mrs C. Day, of Scotts Farm Road, West Ewell.

The bride was attacked by Carol Lyons, Fiona Lynch, Kerry Burden and Karen Gibbs. The best man was Paul Palmer.

Epsom & Ewell Herald

As one might expect with maternity, more women than men have been in-patients.

Daily Telegraph

PROPOSALS to tighten the law on street prostitution and kerb-crawling drivers who harass women are no solution to t h e growing London menace, says Tory MP for Westminster, John Wheeler.

His constituency includes glas sbowl with a live goldfish.

Evening Standard

PROFESSIONAL, 29 years, asian, gentleman, seeks female friends (platonic), any nationality for socialising and evenings out. Box 28B.

Ms London

Beating has been a pleasant river recreation on The Tone for the last three years and Taunton Deane Borough Council would like to see it continued.

Taunton & Bridgwater Shopper

Heart-lung swap woman on menu

Dundee Courier

ONE Orgasm Bag, colour tan £5. — Tel: . .....

Bury Free Press

I, P.J. Visser of 38 De Witte-brug Court, Florida Park hereby give notice that I will not be held responsi-ble for any debts incurred by my wife Debra Estelle Visser (Trollop)

Johannesburg Star

Princess Di stalked by sex perverts

PRINCESS DI is being relentlessly pursued by a pack of perverts — and the royal security force seems powerless to stop them.

While she was enjoying the championship tennis matches at Wimbledon, police spotted a crowd of 18 "dirty old men" who were leering lasciviously at the pregnant princess.

This is only the latest in a series of indignities — and potentially life-threatening situations — the Princess of Wales has been forced to endure.

Police nab 18 'dirty old men' in raincoats

CRUISE
ON WINDERMERE
with Cyril Smith

Book your tickets now,
space is limited!
Saturday, May 30th
Depart Lakeside 6.15 p.m.

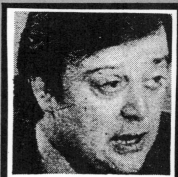

Kenneth Clarke

All-clear for AIDS suspect

Daily Post

● Lesbian, 35, nonsmoker, loves horses seeks same for friendship.

Spare Rib

Golf handicap

An Elsan chemical toilet has disappeared from a hut at Corton's pitch and putt course. Lowestoft police are investigating the theft, but say they have nothing to go on.

Eastern Evening News

REMEMBER

When replying to advertisements it would help us and the advertiser if you would kindly mention.

THE

as the source of your enquiry.

Wimbledon & Morden Guardian

NEW Mobile Home on quiet park, adjacent to shops in Wootton Bassett, suit couple or simple person, pets welcome, £9,850. — Tel. Swindon

Bristol Evening Post

CRIMINAL CHARGES BROUGHT AGAINST STRIKERS AND SUPPORTERS DURING NUM STRIKE

OFFENCE	No. of chges
Murder	3
Assault causing grevious bodily harm	39
Assault causing actual bodily harm	429
Assaulting a police constable	360
Possessing an offensive weapon	49
Riot	137
Unlawful assembly	509
Affray	21
Conduct conductive to a breach of the peace (section 5, Public Order Act 1936)	4107
Breach of the peach	207

The Times

Flying pig

A pig fell from a lorry on the M5 near Exeter and landed on the car bonnet of secretary Linda Hogg, aged 34. The pig was killed.

Western Daily Press

ALARM cloak, Big ben repeater, £4; Small gilt clock, 7 jewels, Wesclox £4. — Bexhill

The Hastings Channel 5 Champion

SUNNY FLAT, W14 Large room. 1/2 poof males. CH/ TV/ Vid phone. £250pcm 493   9-6pm

The Times

BAR FOOD

IN our story on London Hosts, the Grand Met managed house operation, it was stated that the "Pub 80" concept probably appealed more to the younger drinker or those looking for bad food.

This should, of course, have read "Bar food". We apologize for any embarrassment caused.

Morning Advertiser

11,949 people sharing a bath and inside toilet

Islington Neighbourhood News

U.K. official on trial

LONDON, Jan. 29.—A senior Defence Ministry official, accused of leaking secrets on the sinking of the Argentine cruiser to General Belgrano, an Opposition Labour politician, went on trial yesterday, reports UPI.

Statesman (Calcutta)

FOUND Tuesday, 26 February, black and white female kitchen wearing collar. — Apply 8 Mafeking

Champion Shopper

Alone

Mrs Backhouse, 37, and her two children, Harry, 10 and Sophie, 77, were on holiday last night.

Daily Express

It also prohibits youth under 18 from working in or frequenting these "entertainment" businesses, bans streetside solicitors who tempt passersby with visions of carnal delights, and gives the police more authority to shut down transgressors.

The Telegraph, Calcutta

ALMOST 1,000 miles will soon have been walked by 12 regulars from The Crimshaw Pub in Shipley. The 12 men are taking part in a staggered sponsored walk from Ilkley to Bowness

Bradford & Shipley Target

LADIES' sheepskin goat, dark brown, size 12, as new, £48. —

Channel 5 Champion, Hastings

Term of abuse

Sir, — The Guardian should be aware that "Viets" (as in "Viets poised," front page, February 15) is not an acceptable term. It continues to be used as a pejorative statement, analogous to "Japs," "Negroes" or "Pakis," etc.

Dora Nipp.
Toronto, Ontario.

The Grauniad

The Stowe-educated Phillips, who served in the Coldstream Guards during the war, died in 1980. Intriguingly, he went on to marry Georgina Wernher, the daughter of

The Times

Ladbrokes, the race sponsors, have made Oxford favourites at 2-1 on and Cambridge 6-4 against, which hints at a close race. Oxford turned the early tide in their favour when Graham Jones and Bill Lang, both post-graduate Glues, announced their intention to compete.

The Times

Urgent discussions on milk quota rules, of vital interest to EEC West Germany, Italy and France tried to resolve their differences over 600-million gallons of surplus wind produced each year.

The Times

Perhaps the only disappointment of the championships from the British point of view was the defeat of Ade Mafe in the 200 metres at the hands of that good American sprinter Mel Lattany. It was in this Cosford stadium this time last year that Ade first hit the headlines by eating Lattany but yesterday he was not mentally tuned for another big race so soon after his silver medal performance in the world indoor games in Paris last weekend.

Observer

MR. ROBERT BULL AND MISS SUZANNE BULLOCK

The engagement is announced between Robert, son of Mr. and Mrs. Graham Bull, Laurels Farm, Hitcham, and Suzanne, daughter of Mr. and Mrs. Keith Bullock, Church Farm, Cotton.

East Anglian Daily Times

A £10 million reservoir complex on Bodmin Moor, the three-mile long Colliford Lake, was opened yesterday by Mr Ian God, Housing Minister.

Daily Telegraph

When the Queen Mother became a widow so comparatively early in life she though she would retire entirely from public view. But slowly her friends persuaded her to take on appointments and duties again. Once her daughter had been drowned she started to accept invitations and now, although an octogenarian, she is busier than ever.

MALVERN councillors may be increasing their knowledge on the problems of glue sniffing.

Worcester and District Health Authority has offered to give a special talk on the problem and Malvern Hills Council's public health committee will decide today whether to take it up.

Worcester Evening News

SURGEONS' DRIVE TO CUT BACKLOG

Two surgeons at Selly Oak Hospital, Birmingham, plan to keep two operating theatres running none hours a day for three days a week until 300 of the most urgent operations have been carried out.

Daily Telegraph

Gabon crackdown on prostitution

LIBREVILLE (Gabon) — President Omar Bongo, in a crackdown on prostitution, has told police to round up prostitutes and give them to the troops.

"When they have had five or six soldiers on top of them, these women will understand that you mustn't street walk in Gabon," Mr Bongo was quoted as saying in *L'Union* yesterday. — Sapa-Associated Press.

Johannesburg Star

A PROPOSED alcoholics centre in Freemantle has been given the go-ahead ... by Southampton Council's magazine Now. And local Tories are furious because the planning committee will not be considering the issue until Thursday.

The row began when Councillor **Louis Lush**, a leading opponent of the centre, was

Southern Evening Echo

10.0   MORNING WORSHIP. 11.0 LINK.
11.30 A BIT ON THE SIDE.
12.0   WEEKEND WORLD. The State of Thatcherism after the Parkinson affair.
1.0   p.m. POLICE 5. With Shaw Taylor.

Daily Express

Launch of sheath containing spermicide

The Times

Warner Lambert today launches a teaser poster for its Lifestyle sheath. Using a new claim, 'The male contraceptive women will prefer', it precedes a major push.

Gillian Upton

Marketing

England. When she pegged out her drawers on the line she used to say she was washing the curtains of her master's pleasure. The baby grew up to be a grand lad and a great comfort to her, though she once arrived on the doorstep in a fine lather after finding a used conservative in his pencil-box.

Spectator

Africa's birth rate is the world's highest (the only continent reporting a rising average rate of population growth) and its use of coontraceptives is the lowest of any continent. At the projected

Irish Times

Exhibition of rare French letters

Express News Service

Bangalore, Nov 23: The Department of Karnataka State Arc-

Deccan Herald

McBroom, arrested and jailed last February in a crack-down on corruption shortly after the military regime took power in a bloodless coup, hugged and killed U.S. officials who were in court to hear the verdict in her trial

The Japan Times

If the FDP, which recently hanged leaders in an attempt to gain appeal as a centrist party for big business and the self-employed, fails to reach the 5 per cent needed for representation, Chancellor Kohl could eventually be forced to call off the conservative-liberal alliance at national level ahead of the 1987 general election.

Grauniad

SHEEP ATTACKS ROCKET

Sevenoaks News in Focus

'The Love Ban

 11.35pm–1.15am

Birth control comedy. John Cleese scores in a small role.

TV Times

THOMPSON. — Memories today of a dearly loved husband, dad and grandad, John George, on this his 75th birthday. — Always remembered by his loving wife and family.

A bouquet of roses just for you,
Sprinkled with tear drops instead of dew,
And in the mddle a forget me not,
To say dead dad we haven't forgot.   17PC

Hartlepool Mail

A man sought for interview in connection with the shooting of Yorkshire police dog handler Kenneth Oliver was named by detectives today as Barry Peter Edwards, also known as Barry Peter Edwards,

Western Evening Herald

The Queen and the Prince cruised on the river in the yacht, Fairy, and later, at the Town Hall, the Queen knighted the Mayor of Liverpool, Mr. John Bent.

Although Sassoon did not die until 1967, it is his war poems for which he is best remembered.

n 1918 he produced "Counter Attack," a fierce attack on all concerned with the war, except for the fighting hen.

Daily Telegraph

TWO COOKS required immediately for Winkfield Place Cookery College near Windsor. Berks. Must have good qualifications and at least three years experience in catering for numbers of up to 100 Split shifts. Monday Friday Might suit 2 friends. Single room accommodation available. Salary negotiable depending on experience. Telephone Miss Grubb on

The Times

Weather reports depress potatoes

By Our Commodities Staff

ATO PRICES fell back ly on the London futures

Financial Times

AIDS cases may reach a million health chief says

**By Thomson Prentice
Science Correspondent**

There could be a million cases of the killer desease AIDS, Acquired Immoral Deficiency Syndrome, worldwide by the end of the century, and known cases in Britain have risen dramatically since the beginning of this year, a senior health executive said yesterday

The Times

GENUINE FAKE FURS AT GENUINE LOW PRICES
ONLY £19.95 + £2.05 p&p
Style and Comfort with that look of real mink

Grauniad

<u>Directions to Sheppey General Hospital</u>

Having crossed over the bridge on the
Island link road (A249) turn right at the
roundabout along the A250, second left
along Scocles Road and bear left at the
end along the one way street system.
After about 50 years, cross over the main
Minster Road and proceed up Waterloo Hill
(Union Road) bear left at the top into
Wards Hill Road and the main entrance to
the hospital

One-legged escapee rapist still on run

The Weekend Australian

Teachers hang five over action

Cambridge Evening News

THE Irish Stammerers' Association will hold a seminar will hod a seminar entited "Aids for Stammerers" tonight

The Irish Press

Lovely furnished modern mobile hole, select site, Residential or holidays. Overlooking Aberystwyth and sea.—Phone 0970   P41

Cambrian News

The announcement of the disqualification was greeted by booze from spectators at the pool.

Gloucestershire Echo

THOROUGHBRED FILLY. 2 years old, for sale, by Shit in the Corner out of Lady Dromara. approximately 15.2 years old, for sale, by Sit

Dumfries & Galloway Standard

STUFFED NUN............£0.90
(Stuffed with potatoes and spices)

Royal Bengal Tandoori Restaurant Woodbridge

● John Wright hit 55 off 44 balls but New Zealand failed by five runs to overhaul Pakistan's total of 157 for five in 20 years

Grauniad

CHÓIR: The annual meeting of Penybontfawr Male Voice Choir was presided over by Mr S. O. Tanat Richards, who had been chairman of the Choir up to the time of his death in 1983.

Mid-Wales County Times & Express

A STUDY by the Building Research Establishment of when and how much people open office windows shows window opening is dependent on the weather.

Building Design

9.0 Lyn Marshall's Everyday Yoga

A sequence of yoga movements that builds up day-by-day into a routine that will stretch and exercise the entire body. 15: *The Leg Over*

Radio Times

GREENWOLD, Florence May. – Late of 163 Bergholt Road, Colchester. A simple, kind, and loving old lady who died with great dignity at 'Ambleside', Wood Lane, Fordham Heath, Colchester on Saturday, April 3, 1982 at 3.10pm. Loved by family and friends who knew her will.

Essex County Standard

Blk 2 Shaukaiwan R/E 5-52
Fuk Yiu, 1015 King's Rd 5-6120
Fuk Yiu Kwan 5-66

Hong Kong Telephone Directory

Give you a certain way to release the suffering from rheumatism arthristis, sore bone and bumbness. If you contact our association K691038 K7114192 from morning time to 12:30 am.

South China Morning Post

50 KING EDWARD Invisible cigars £25 or will sell in packets of 5 £2.80 ea.   after 6 p.m.
BEAUTIFUL Berketex off the

Merseymart

Labour whip opposes cane

Timed Ed. Supplement

AKVINA BODEGRAVEN HOLLAND

Confiture - Strawberries

مـربى الـفراولـة

المكونات فراولة ـ سكر ـ مواد حافظة مرخصة

Ingrs.: Sugar - Strawberries - Conservatives

Jam label

She went on: "I guess our marriage was beginning to disintegrate about a year and a half before we parted. A lot of it had to do with a midwife crisis because George was not working at the time.

Manchester Evening News

RAPIST, E. F. Dickson, M.N.C.P., day or evening apointments. — Tel. 01-   (LTC) A2

LIES! LIES! LIES! —PAGES 4 AND 5

The Sun

Another heavily-backed horse was Church Parade, owned by the Queen. But housewives who rushed to back the horse with the royal wedding in mind to see Church Parade finish were disappointed.

The Queen was at the course well back in fifth place.

Daily Mail

Roger Scruton

Keep this monster in its grave

The Times

---

sic
Music for Palm Sunday, Cantores Mundi, Notre Dame de France, Leicester Place, off Leicester Square, 4.30.
BBC Sympathy Orchestra, *Elijah*, by Mendelssohn, Albert Hall, 7.30.

The Times

I'M looking for a kind home for my 15.1 heavyweight Cob Gelding, he's quiet in every way, but gay, £700 o.n.o. — Exeter █████, Monday.

Western Morning News

GUERNSEY cow, freshly carved, quiet, used to being hand milked. — Guildford ███████.   L4546

Haslemere Herald

BRA shoot on Saturday

Barbados Advocate

JEMMETT. — Cast away at his home, Culcraggie. Alness.

The Scotsman

Great radio comedy hit shows including Bandwagon, Much Binding, Take It from Archie, Hancock, Round the Here, The Goons, Educating Horne, I'm Sorry, I'll Read That Again, will be recalled in The Comedy Years, on Radio 4 in October.

Guardian

National Tyre Service has announced the appointment of F G Skidmore as general manager of its garage equipment company based in Northampton.

■ Mrs Thatcher ■ Mr Pym

WEDDING IS POSTPONED

Torquay Herald Express

1978 Fish Van with scales, £600. Tel Fleetwood

Evening Gazette

**A HEALING SESSION
by John Cain
(of Birkenhead)**

★

Owing to illness:
**MEETING
CANCELLED**

Southport Visiter

23, PRETTY PETITE BLOBE, seeks attractive male, outgoing 24-31, photo, phone please. Box 361.

Nine to Five

Births

BRATT — On Friday, July 27, to Annette (nee Wray) and Clive — a son (Mark John). Thanks to GP and all at JCMW.

Isle of Man Courier

Tuesday, April 27th
WELSH NATIONAL OPERA "SMETANA" The Battered Bride at **APOLLO THEATRE, OXFORD.** Dep. 5.45 p.m. Fare (inc.) £9.

Henley Standard

PART-TIME
DENTON HALL & BURGIN
SOLICITORS
Seek a POOF READER
for their Word Processing Department.

Standard

2nd Year Cadet

for

**Radio 4MK
Mackay, Queensland**

Must be able to read.

Apply

**GENERAL MANAGER
P.O. Box 183
MACKAY, QLD 4740**

LOST AND FOUND—
FOUND. Two stray Nuns,
mating pair, seen Al-
mondsbury. Phone

The Bristol Gazette

DAD OF THE YEAR COMPETITION

RESULTS

The winner of our recent Dad of the Year Competition is:-

**Miss Stephanie Pardy of
Ridding Close
Shirley
Southampton**

who wins a place in the final of the Dad of the Year
Competition in London in June.

Southern Echo

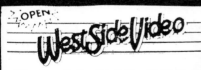

OPEN

WestSide Video

Tel: 01-749 6864

43b Goldhawk Road,
London W12

*FREE LIFE
MEMBERSHIP*
For 1 month only

Uxbridge, Slough & District Recorder

SUCCESSFUL
businessman,
widower, aged 44,
usual trappings, non-
smoker with varied
interests, seeks affec-
tionate, understanding
female to shave the
enjoyable things in
life. Box No. 4881,
Yorkshire Post Ltd.,
Leeds 1.

Yorkshire Post

PEDESTRIANS using the Otley Road to Harlow Car public footpath are being urged to fight for their right to stroll in peace.

According to Mr. Alan Ravenscroft, Harrogate Council's director of parks, people who are terrorised by motorists contravening the "Access Only" signs should make a stand against them and report the offenders' registration number to the police.

At the same time the public should also keep an eye open for vandals who in the past have destroyed wooden "No Access" signs at the start of the footpath forcing the council to erect metal ones instead.

The footpath is a popular one and widely used by mature lovers and dog-walkers alike, especially at weekends.

PLEASE save from destruction, three kitchens in desperate need of good caring homes. — Swansea 54934.

South Wales Evening Post

TEMPORARILY CLOSED DUE TO FIRE.

The PROPRIETOR of BLAZES RESTAURANT, CHARING CROSS, GLASGOW, wishes to APOLO-

Glasgow Herald

It makes me want to wee, when I hear that we are getting a new nine-storey office block on the site of the old Golden Eagle pub in Hill Street.

The building, so we are told, will have a smooth mirror look about it. It will be a building of some distinction, say the architects.

Birmingham Evening Mail

---

5. GDYNIA SPECIAL Holiday ref
INTRODUCTORY OFFER
GDYNIA ORBIS HOTEL ★★★★
GDY-7

Holiday dates:
22-29 Jun
6-13, 20-27 Jul
10-17, 24-31 Aug
7-14 Sep

The prices start from **£79.00** per person in a double room with private facilities
The price includes:
— Bed and breakfast accommodation
— AM Saturday city tour (incl. Gdansk)
— Fight not included

The Spring Fayre for the Home of Rest for Old Horses was held at the Sefton Hotel, Douglas, on Thursday. Pictured are some who attended.

Isle of Man Times

VIOLENT-TEMPERED Russell Harty stood in a street brandishing a carving knife and threatening to kill a man, Gosport magistrates were told today.

Portsmouth Evening News

When it comes to being fatuous

Daily Express

GALE on Friday

COLUMNIST OF THE YEAR

Noisy welcome for prince

Prince Charles, at the controls, circled Victoria Falls before setting his Andover plane down to a noisy welcome from thousands of Africans and British expatriates in Zambia yesterday.

"It's very spectacular. What do you say?. It's very impressive," the prince said later as he stood in a shower of spray watching the tumbling waters of the Zambesi River.

Residents of the area called the falls "Musi-o-Tunya," which means "the smoke that thunders."

The prince, who is on a two-week tour of Africa, visited Tanzania before arriving in Zambia.

The next instalment of our serial will appear on Monday

Dundee Courier & Advertiser

ROYAL GRAMM\.R SCHOOL
Guildford
(700 boys 11-18)

Required in January, 1984
A PART-TIME

TEACHER OF MAOOOOOOOO"

Approximately 3½ days per week.

Camberley News & Mail

Awards to writers

By Dennis Barker

Farrukh Dhondy, a 40-year-old Indian bor in Poona, yesterday won the Samuel Beckett Award

Grauniad

DAFT regulations for a scheme to give council house tenants a right to repair their own homes and then be re-imbursed by their landlords have been issued by the Government.

Tiverton Gazette

Queen Elizabeth walked one block to King's Saddlery, where she spent over 45 minutes, bought a belt, a pair of gloves and some raiding equipment

Trinidad Guardian

Coun. Blackman said: "It's a great honour to have a French warship in our marina.

"I'm looking forward to visiting her. I've never been on a French warship or one of any kind since I left the Royal Navy."

Coun. Blackman was a pretty officer in destroyers, based at Portsmouth.

MOTORING organisations criticised Britain's top price motorway petrol station yesterday for selling 4-star at £189·9p a gallon.

Resident Assistant Caretaker

Kilburn area — Ref: KI/245
Wages: £89.44 per week

The successful applicant will work as part of a team in the above area and will be expected to carry out normal caretaking and cleaning duties and be the Council's representative on the Estate, particularly outside office hours to provide help and assistance to the tenants, for which Rent and Rat free accommodation will be given.

Accommodation will be given on a Service Tenancy basis (normally a two bedroomed flat). 39 hours per week

This post is NOT suitable for job sharing

 THOMAS TRAVEL

HOLIDAYS

TWO WEEK SPECIAL HOLIDAY

FROM

CHIPPENHAM TO YUGOSLAVIA

DEPART SUNDAY 26th MAY 1985

PRICE £263.00

THIS INCLUDES:-

TRANSFER FROM CHIPPENHAM TO LONDON (HEATHROW) AND BACK. FLIGHT TO SPLIT
2 WEEKS ACCOMMODATION IN THE HOTEL LAV

The man is slim, around 5 ft 7 ins tall with brown, shoulder-length hair. He also has a beard, which would make him noticeable if he was wearing a dress.

Anyone who can help the police should call Hackney police station, telephone 488 7111.

Hackney Gazette

CAPRICORN (Dec. 22-Jan. 20) Confidence will be on the increase now and make it easier to obtain your objectives. Uranus is also in action and touched by Lady Luck.

Scottish Daily Record

Helicopter saves Jeremy Thorpe trapped in cove

The Times

God, who was transferred from Manchester City to Rotherham on the same day that Doyle moved, was also dismissed in his second match in new colours.

Scottish Daily Record

Hardworking & Conscious
SECRETARY

with a pleasant personality, to work for 2 partners in a specialist West End accountancy practice.

Limited secretarial duties
Busy shorthand
Some accounts
Lively telephone

The Standard

Prince Henry's family can be traced back to 620 and originated in Saoie, South-East France, where they were the "Soulerain Seigneurs" of Haute Savoie. The Prince, a public relations consultant, lied in London from 1948 until 1965 when he retired to Ireland.

Daily Telegraph

HOLIDAYS

COULD YOU TURN a slightly shabby country flat in the heart of the Lake District into a home? Two double bedrooms, very large living-room, big bathroom and kitchen. Mod cons and own stream. £30 a week, seducing in winter.

Out West

GREG NORMAN, hot favourite for the Card Classic at Royal Porthcawl, missed a five-inch putt on the 11th green yesterday.

The blind Australian tried to tap in the tiddler one-handed but hit the ground with his putter and only just moved the ball.

Sporting Life

8.20pm BBC2 1911: A year in Musical History. Gustav Mahler died in 1911 in Vienna aged fifty, leaving two works complete but unperformed - The Ninth Symphony and the Dong of the Earth.

Hampstead Local Advertiser

In a letter to the NEWS Mrs Irene Mahadur, of Percy Road, Ore, said she and a friend were walking in Clifton Road, Ore, a few weeks ago. 'We had the horrible experience of witnessing a large rat about the size of a large kitchen emerge from the litter bin outside the staff entrance to the geriatric side of St Helen's Hospital.

Hastings News

Muffins and music

"I think people are looking for a quality of life, a return to the old standards and that is what we intend to give them," he mused.

Quality at the Waldorf tea dance costs £4¹.95 a head. For that one gets sandwiches, muffins, cakes and scones, a choice of Indian or China tea, and the opportunity to meet what Mr McHardy calls "the right sort of person."

The quartet led by Mrs Eddie Strevens on the sexophone plays old favourites in every tempo from the waltz to the tango.

Daily Telegraph

HACKNEY: A good example of a Labour borough where the old guard has been ousted by newt Left-wingers.

DESSERT:
Creme-de-Menthe and Chocolate Mousse
OR
Raspberry Pavlova
———— :: ————
Cheeseboard with Celery and Gropes
———— :: ————
Ground Coffee with Cream and Mints
———— :: ————

Somerset Standard

In our report of a meeting of Wexford Corporation, published on May 5, it was stated that Sean Finn, Seamus Swan and James Kavanagh, all from Wexford, had been convicted on the attempted murder of an English-born hotel owner.

This was incorrect. The three were in fact convicted of possession of fire arms with intent to endanger life, control of fire-arms with intentn to endanger life, unlawfully and maliciously shooting with intent to cause grievous bodily harm, unlawfully and maliciously shooting with intent to maim and maliciously wounding. We apologise to the three men.

Evening Press (Dublin)

THORNHILL: Fully fitted ground floor modern Flatlet. Ideal for a single person. Entrance vestibule, loving room, complete with fold down bed and wardrobes, fully fitted kitchen, cooker, refrigerator, automatic washing machine, tumble dryer, tiled bathroom, Avocado suite, every conceivable extra included. Lounge suite and pine furniture, fitted carpets, blinds, even lampshades. Car standing, move straight in. **£18,995.** (2373)

Advertisement/South Wales Echo

Welsh gold has been minced for decades, but big extraction companies have surveyed the area and decided there is not enough to justify mining operations.

The Times

1   **Births**

HOEKSTRA. — Bob and Sue (nee Atkinson) are proud to announce the birth of their son Paul on Friday 2nd April at St. Augustine's Hospital. Thanks be unto God for His unspeakable gift.

Daily News (S. Africa)

APOLOGY

Due to a typographical error in last week's issue of the **Enfield Independent**, the words 'Con-Men' appeared on the border of **Ashley & Nephews** advertisement. 'Con-Men' was the headline of a story that was not used because of lack of space and is absolutely nothing to do and is in no way connected with **Ashley & Nephews**.

We apologise for any inconvenience or embarrassment caused by this unfortunate error and would like to make it clear that **Ashley & Nephews** are a well established and highly respectable company and are North London's largest suppliers of aids for the disabled.

The Enfield Independent

6 0 THE SCENT OF MAN. 7 : The Majestic Clockwork. Dr Bronowski's re-run series looks at the revolution in scientific thought brought about by Einstein's theory of relativity.

Grauniad

THE Yorkshire ribber Peter Sutcliffe yesterday lost an attempt to stop him being made a bankrupt

Grauniad

CLERGYMAN ON SEX CHARGES

The Rev John Vile, of Robin's Lane, Barry, South Glamorgan, was charged yesterday with three offences of gross indecency

Daily Telegraph

Harbans Singh d e s e r v e s credit for the selection of stories which are practically among the classics in Punjabi short fiction and are marked for, as the blurb says its "high literary excellence." The translation is in impoccable English,

Art of Living

Mrs Williams, daughter of the 1920s feminist and pacifist campaigner Vera Brittain, is a 512-year-old Roman Catholic whose marriage was legally dissolved.

Her appearance is rumpled, if not dishevelled, and she has a reputation for being late for appointments.

Arab Times

During the case the prosecution "lost" five witnesses: one man was shot dead, another stabbed to death, a woman prostitute was hacked to death, another woman died of a heroin overdose and another man died of drink. But police were satisfied there were no suspicious circumstances, the court heard.

The Standard

In a radio interview aimed at Latin America and circulated to stations there yesterday Mrs Thatcher singled out oil exploration, fisheries and toryism as three fields for expansion.

Daily Telegraph

THREE ADMIT INDECENCY CHARGE

THREE MEN, all in their 60's, were found by police committing indecent acts with each other in public toilets at Northville Road, Filton, a court heard this week.

Mr. Miles described the offences as 'at the bottom end of the scale' of seriousness.

North Avon Gazette

After the guests were presented to Queen Elizabeth and the Duke of Edinburgh, King Hussein and Queen Noor, the hosts chatted with guests without formality which gave an ambiance of simplicity and sent the guests home with a feeling having attended an unforgivable event.

It was the first state banquet at Windsor since one for Denmark's Queen Margrethe in 1974.

Mr Reagan sat between the Queen and her sister Princess Margaret Thatcher.

Majorca Daily Bulletin

The dead and wounded were sitting in cafes on the town's main street early on Sunday, contemplating the day while the town's Maronite Christians attended mass at the church of St Eli.

Grauniad

Fierce hitting by Rodney Ontong helped to balance periods of inactivity by Francis, who was eventually run out at 150. A six in the final over by Ontong helped Glamorgan to reach 170-4 when their innings closed after 45 years.

South Wales Echo

London: The Coach House, 3 Hermitage, Westwood Park SE23; walled courtyard and roof gardens, pants for sale, sculptor's studio, sculpture and paintings for sale — percentage for charity; 2 to 6.30.

The Times

Mrs Kate Wood, 30, a social worker and daughter of a local gamekeeper, was chatting with a friend on the telephone yesterday lunchtime, when a sinister stooping figure emerged from a corpse about 60 yards from her cottage.

Daily Telegraph

Intruder scare

A youth was recently discovered to have entered the private bathroom of Countless Spencer, stepmother of the Princess of Wales.

The Grauniad

BBC move will restore cuts on Radio 3

By David Hewson
Arts Correspondent

The British Braodcasting Corporation is to extend broadcasting to 17 hours a day, seven days a week, from Saturday, restoring the cuts in its hours made in 1980, and putting the newtwork on the air for the longest time each week in its history.

The Times

Ward sister slashed

A SISTER at Whiston Hospital was viciously attacked while on ward duty in the early hours of Sunday morning.

The incident happened at 2.10am when the sister was going to the ladies toilet at the burns unit.

the toilet, sprang out and slashed her arm with a knife.

THERE'S an unmentionable four-letter word in Northern Ireland's World Cup vocabulary at the moment .. defeat.

Daily Mirror

Anna, who drew the picture, and Dave, who wrote the words, were chosen out of more than 300 entries by judges, CND chairman Joan Ruddock, illustrator Raymond Briggs and advertising agency director Johnny Wright.

They will receive their prize the GLC leader Ken Livingstone at County Hall on October 8.

The Standard

While sympathising with the miners and arguing the British government could have acted to end the strike, Jessica Larive-Groenendaal (Neth) said she and her Liberal colleagues could not support a strike called without a ballet

European Parliament News

NORMAN St John Stevas is one of the bent-known Catholic politicians in modern Britain. He has been Leader of the House of Commons, Chancellor of the Duchy of Lancaster and Minister for the arts. He was

Irish Independent

● Sutton United Supporters FC, who play in the Morden 'and District League, require players for all positions to strengthen the tea' for this season.

Sutton and Cheam Herald

Liberal MP Clement Fraud, also one of the speakers at the opening, said it was an exciting development for this corner of London and all that was needed now was "people with a little money in their pockets" to enjoy the smell of its success.

Richmond and Twickenham Times

SINNER SUIT, tailor made, chest 38in., inside leg 29in., £80. 041
SWEDISH lamb jacket and

Glasgow Herald

Jackie's style costs her £30m

Best-selling novelist Jackie Collins' reputation for racy writing has cost her a staggering £30 million.

An appeal court in New York threw out the award she won from a now — defunct magazine which incorrectly put her name under a picture of a topless woman.

A three-man panel in Manhattan said that Mrs. Collins — sister of actress Joan "by voluntarily devoting herself to the public's interest in sexual mores" did not deserve full protection of her privacy.

The case began four years ago when the U.S. Magazine Adelina published a topless picture which was a still from the movie "The World is Full of Married Men," written by Jackie Collins

The woman in the picture was identified as Ms. Collins and a jury later awarded her 40 million dollars. The trial judge later reduced this to 10 million.

Yesterday the appeals panel quashed the award and said: "By voluntarily devoting herself to the public's interest in sexual hores through extensive writing on this topic, reaping profits and wide notoriety for herself in the process, she must be deemed to have surrendered what would have been her protectable privacy."

Judge Richard Gardamore said Ms. Collins own works are "full of descriptions of sex and orgies an are heavily laden with four-latter words. She admits they are considered pornographic."

He added. "Given the number of famous persons portrayed in this fashion (nude) one wonders whether such pictures are even capable of producing genuine reputational harm."

Dublin Evening Press

GAMES, as new: Contraception, £3; Mouse Trap, £3; Stay Alive, £3; Connect Four, £2. — Sheffield 3.....

Doncaster Star

Man assists police in rape of nurse

Trinidad and Tobago Express

In 1975 charitable contributions from private individuals amounted to nearly a third of charities' total income. Now they are estimated to account for little more than a tent,

The Times

MALE HIPPY — headbanger, 23, seeks other males, any age — any sex — into almost everything. Please write Box No. 228.

MARRIAGES

BANKS—MARTIN: D'CRUZ — On September 29th, 1984, quietly in bath, Richard to Yvonne.

The Times

PETS

WIFE 41YRS, 5'9", Good cook, snappy dresser, bad time keeper, attractive Low cost runner, goes well. Will swap for boat or negotiable price.

GrinstAD

Pardon sought

Geoffrey Davis, formerly Mycock, aged 38, freed after serving 16 years of a life sentence for murder has said he will not stop until he secures a pardon **Page 3**

The Times

● A deception from Durham County Council is to meet NCB chairman Ian MacGregor in London on Monday to discuss the future of opencast coal mining in the county.

Durham Advertiser

LIVERPOOL HEALTH AUTHORITY
Mersey Regional Health Authority
CONSULTANT PSYCHIATRIST
Drug Dependent
Whole-Time or Maximum Part Time
This is a newly created post, which will provide the

British Medical Journal

BARNES. Just in the market! Newly refurn hse of character in the fashionable Merthyr Terrace. Just 7 miles walk from tube.

Sunday Times

HARRY'S A HIT
IN LIVESTOCK
SHOW LISTS

By far the commonest name in the record entry of livestock for this year's Royal Smithfield Show is "Harry" following the birth of Prince Henry.

There are a score or more Harrys listed in the various classes and many other names are linked to the prince, such as Wee Harry, Prince Charming, Charlie's Boy and Donington Harry.

The show, which takes place at Earl's Court in December, is the shop window for Britain's agriculture and attracts visitors from all over the world including many official government and trade missions.

red underpants and a digital watch.

Daily Telegraph

'Fine cut'
costs Mercedes
driver a
£25 fine

A MIDDLETOWN lorry driver who admitted a careless driving charge at Tuesday's Magistrates Court in Armagh, was fined £25 by R.M. Mr G. Harty.

Colm Mullan (37) of Ivy Park was stated to have caused a police cat to swerve as he drove his Mercedes car around a bend. on the Monaghan/Middletown Road on July 7th.

Ulster Telegraph

LYCEUM THEATRE
Heath Street, Crewe.
Telephone 211149

WEEK COMMENCING
MONDAY, 24th SEPT.

Nightly 7.45   Sat. 5 p.m. & 8 p.m.

GRANADA TV FAVOURITE
DAPHNE OXENFORD
IN THE DELIGHTFUL COMEDY FOR ALL
THE FAMILY

BUTTERFLIES ARE FREE
BY LEONARD GERSHE
* TWO SEATS FOR THE PRICE OF
ONE ON MONDAY *
CONFESSIONS FOR OAPs/CHILD/
STUDENTS/NURSES/UNWAGED ON
TUES/WED/THURS.

10.15 A Book at Bedtime: 'Some Do
Not' by Fred Madox Ford.
Abridged in 15 parts (13). Read
by Hugh Burden. 10.29 Weather.
10.30 The World Tonight, incl 11.00

Radio Times

HARVEST gold luxury Bathroom Suite, twin grip bath
complete with panel, taps,
symphonic wc, suite, vanity
unit with bowl and taps,
£500. Half-price at £250 inc
VAT.

New chief

SCOTLAND YARD have set a spy catcher on Hampstead's burglars.

For the new chief of the Metropolitan Police's Hampstead Division is 41 year-old Chief Supt. Peter Bettany who was convicted at the Old Bailey earlier this year.

Camden New Journal

WEST Hampstead's police threw open their doors to hoardes of visitors for the first time in five years last Friday and Saturday.

On Friday parties of school children were given the opportunity to help solve a murder, have their finger prints taken or incur horrible mick injuries.

Hampstead Local Advertiser

SKIRT, all wool, waist 32/34, length 28", suit elderly lad, box pleated, £1.50. 32 Albany Drive, Herne Bay, eves.

Adscene (Canterbury)

PROPERTY OF THE MONTH
£35,250 WEYMOUTH CLOSE, CHERITON — Almost attractive and well maintained semi-detached bungalow

MERMAID or Merman wanted to sit among fish and look petty. £10 for 3 hours' work on Lewes night December 6th. — Phone The Ark Seafood Shop, Lewes 476912.

Sussex Express

James Thin, Kenneth Warren

**House of Commons (Services):
Library Sub-Committee**
Committee Clerk, Mr Pamphlett

Vacher's Parliamentary Companion

on 471231 (Ref. RHL).
EXPERIENCED & WILLING relief goat milder required for 2 B.S. Goats in Seaford, good pay and free mild. Seaford 89
FULL OR PART TIME, enthusiastic

Friday-Ad

```
We stand for:-

*    An end to racism and discrimination
     in jobs, housinf, education and social
     services.  Decent services for all !!

*    Jobs for all, black and white !!

*    A 35 hour wee, with no loss in pay !!

*    A £100 a week national minimum wage !!

*    Abolition of all immigration controls.
     Repeal the Nationality and Immigration
     Acts !!
```

Liverpool Labour Party leaflet

OBITUARY
SIR LEONARD SINCLAIR
Fifty years in petroleum

The Times

Japanese to scrub Turkish baths

From Robert Whymant in Tokyo

Earlier, the Turkish embassy here had complained to the Foreign Ministry about the constant phone calls from me wanting to book a massage.

The Grauniad

ARCHDEACON DIES IN HIS STALL

Church Times

New Deaths

There are people dying this year who never died before," reported an Irish coroner.

Times of India

Lendl was seen at his spectacular best in the final. Wembley has never seen more violent serving. Lendl conceded only 15 points against service in the match

Yorkshire Post

Labour-Chef Neil Kinnock

MARY NUTTER
Psychometry, Tarot, Healing

Whatever your problem I can
give you Psychic Advice
from your letter

But if you don't really want
the truth don't waste your
money, or my time

**FEE £2 per question
Absent Healing Free**

Plus s.a.e. to
Box A29
c/o Prediction

Prediction

Singing threat for the pensioners

FERNHILL Senior
Citizens were enter-
tained last Monday
afternoon by the loc-
al Reuther Choir.

Rutherglen Reformer

BMW Executive car of the '80s

Malawi Phone Directory

For Immediate Release.

On October 1st at 12 noon, April Ashley, one of the first people in Britain to have had a sex-change operation, will be at the Edinburgh Tapestry Company (Dovecot Studios) to take part in a cutting-off ceremony.

Press Release

ROYAL COLLEGE OF SURGEONS OF ENGLAND

Examinations Clerk

Required to assist in the administration of medical examinations and to shame other general duties.

Applicants are expected to have an educational background. Up to degree level and/or relevant work experience.

The work demands a conscientious and methodical approach to paperwork coupled with the ability to deal personally with examiners and candidates, and work as part of a busy team. Typing/keyboard skills essential. Salary £5670-£7404 plus £1042 London Weighting (under review).

Apply in writing with curriculum vitae to Personnel Officer, Royal College of Surgeons of England from whom further particulars will be available. Closing date September 28.

The Standard

Brinks ,,open hearth'' stove

There is nothing as cosy as a Brink open hearth. Used either as an open fire or as a stove, it takes coal, wood, anthracite or coallite, and brings back almost forgotten feelings of well-being during the long and chilly winter evenings.

Although from a finer mould, but just as strong and robust as the series bigger Brink stoves, this stove is particularly suitable for smaller rooms.

It has two plates on top that provide economical and practical comfort.

A singing cattle and an inviting pot of fresh coffee brings back the nostalgic atmosphere of old.

And what could be nicer than to spend a happy hour after school gathered around the glowing stove with children having a cup of steaming chocolate.

Advertising leaflet

HOLIDAY FIRM COLLAPSES

A liquidator was called in yesterday at Ventura Holidays, which has offices in London, Manchester and Sheffield. The hundreds of holidaymakers currently abroad with the firm have been guaranteed a free journey home.

The Civil Aviation Authority said: "We will try to get everyone home with as little convenience as possible."

Daily Telegraph

MR. SPEAKER: Order.

MRS. CHINAMANO: Cde. Speaker, he
started saying I was a bitch. That is why I
answered him thus and said that he is the son of
a bitch and the son of a homosexual. He must
withdraw saying that I am a bitch first, and then
I will withdraw after that. You must not be biased.

Debate in House of Assembly, Zimbabwe

> ..ED LOBBYING ... BRITISH RAIL TO MAINTAIN
> SERVICES TO BRADFORD.
>
> IT IS UP TO MPs AND COUNCILLORS TO ENSURE THAT BRADFORD RECEIVES
> THE HELP IT NEEDS TO UNDERGO THE INDUSTRIAL REVITALISATION NEEDED
> TO BRING NEW NOBS" SAID MR. LAWLER IN A STATEMENT
>
> GEOFF'S OTHER ACTIVITIES.

Bradford Conservative Party News-Sheet

Reagan and the right

Dennis H. Wrong

TLS

Industries

The main industry is fishing, there are about 30 large cuttters besides a large number of smaller fishing vessels.

Principal catches are shrimps – salmon, Greenland halibut and cod – along with considerable quantities of seal – walrus – whale and reindeer.

Greenland Travel Bureau

Sacked official to join another union

By Norman Crossland

BRISTOL transport union official Mr Paul Chamberlin, sacked after allegations of ballot-rigging, has been accepted as a member of the Amalgamated Engineering Workers' Union.

"I've been proposed and seconded and the Bristol branch has approved," he said.

Mr Chamberlin, who led a Bristol dustmen's dispute last year, was dismissed from his full-time TGWU job.

It was alleged he was involved in ballot-rigging to find a successor to the union's general secretary, Mr Moss Evans.

He described his trade as that of rigger and said he was still unemployed.

Bristol Evening Post

Coun Colin Peacock pointed out: "The chairman is sick of people knocking Miss GB and wonders what we would have left without it. Well, if you get rid of Miss GB, you get rid of the knockers."

The Grauniad

Gun runner

A BELFAST fugitive stole a police machine gun and hijacked two patrol cars before being caught. Police said he had no parliamentary connections.

Northern Echo

tion the woman, who is not being named, will wear a long red raincoat, burgundy boots, a light brown skirt, a tan handbag and light brown gloves similar to those worn by Mr. Maddocks, of Institute Road, King's Heath.

Birmingham Evening Mail

Man jailed following police chase

SERVICE manager Charles Grant, of Newport, who reached speeds of 110mph in his Renault Turbot car while being chased by police, was jailed for 28 days last week.

Suffron Waldon Reporter

THE CLEVELAND ARMS
resents entertainment by

BOBBY RAY

On Saturday, March 23

Meals always available. Extension

Telephone
High Ercall 770204

Shropshire Star

Mr Freeson, 59, an ex-Housing Minister, won the seat with a 4,834 majority in a sex-cornered fight at the last election.

Western Daily Press

THE identity of a headless corpse found in a tree in woodland near Liskeard will not be positively known until dental records have been checked.

Police, who have ruled out foul

Western Morning News

Camera may have exposed a fossil

Sir Fred Hoyle

The Grauniad

Poison riddle

A FAMILY of three were seriously ill in hospital last night after being found unconscious by their dead pet dog.

Sunday People

WEST OXFORDSHIRE

Extremely ripe for modernisation

invited for the Freehold.

Offers on £50,000

Oxford Times

with the painter. After the death in 1982 of his wife and muse, Gala, Dali withdrew into isolation, refusing to eat or receive visitors.

The Grauniad

COLMAN—BALLS — The engagement is announced between TIMOTHY, son of Mr. and Mrs. B. P. COLMAN, of 40, Fakenham Road, Drayton, and MARIE, daughter of Mr. and Mrs. R. E. BALLS, of 122, West End, Old Costessey. —Love from both Families.

Eastern Evening News

AIDS threatens heterosexuals

In today's science/medicine pages; Evidence is growing that AIDS can be spread through conventional sexual contact; the world's great coral reefs are endangered.

The Globe and Mail

Close-ups of France

Maud Cottave is a lecturer in sociology at Grenoble University – and one of the minority of the population who was born.

Radio Times

CYCLING HOLIDAYS. Shakespeare country/Cotswolds. Great accom, everything supplied. Penny Farting, 4 Emscote Rd, Warwick CV34 4PP. (0926) 498948.

The Observer

Baker

In a court case in yesterday's T. & A. it was stated that Mr. Gerard Joseph Ronan, of Copyfields, Allerton, Bradford, was a demolition expert. This was incorrect. He is a baker.

Bradford Telegraph & Argus

Le 6 mars 1984, en révélant les objectifs de la restructuration, le président des charbonnages (National Cock Board), M. Ian MacGregor, indiquait qu'il fallait réduire de 4 millions de tonnes la production, qui avait été de 100 millions en 1983. Aujourd'hui, il est pratique-

Le Monde

BOCKING END CONGREGATIONAL CHURCH. – At the bi-monthly social meeting Mrs Edna Hazelwood gave a most enlightening talk entitled Death of a Street when she outlined the history of New Street, Braintree. The subject is one of interest for both newcomers to Braintree and those who have lived here for many years. Following the talk mince pies and tea were served, and then Christmas carols were sung to round off the evening.

Last Sunday morning the service was conducted by the Rev Bryan Tween and after the opening hymn the Sunday school children brought their gifts to be passed on to children in need. The third Advent candle was lit and then the children enacted the Christmas story in a very moving way whilst the choir sang the relevant parts of various carols.

The minister told the children about the legend of the little star and, having read from Luke, chapter two, he reminded the congregation of the booze up and time of great joy which is for everyone.

Braintree and Witham Times

WANTED: Loving home for two young ladies, sweet natured, intelligent, 12 weeks old, part collie. — Gower 39

South Wales Evening Post

ONCE it was thought so powerful and subversive that Queen Victoria refused to have it in the place. Now it's just another Fleet Street newspaper, c o m p l e t e with mipsrints, fighting for circulation.

We are talking, of course, of The Times, 200 years old this week, and the subject of much attention on all TV channels. Last night's Thames

Daily Mail

A perfect end to a perfect meal –
Relax at home with

ANTONIA FRASER

Cllr. D. J. Thomas told a meeting of the council on Monday that the fouling of Aberaeron by dogs had become a desperate situation.

"The town was filthy throughout the summer and it was difficult not to step on dog filth as you walked along the promenade", Cllr. Thomas said.

"Whenever I take my grandchildren to the playing area in Parc-y-Fro, the sand is full of this filth. It is a matter of real concern and I blame incontinent handlers — residents and visitors — for the problem."

The Cambrian News

■ STAND-IN: Former England rugby skipper Steve Smith replaces the injured Nigel Melville as scum half

Daily Mirror

Bury 2
West Ham United 2

When the first division leaders meet a fourth division team, even quite a good one, they are expected to win. West Ham duly did so last night,

The Times

10.10 WORD CINEMA. Black God, White Devil (1964). Brazilian film starring Maurício de Valle and Geraldo del Rey, which follows the extraordinary odyssey of a man who becomes involved with two bandits, one black, one white (not in colour).

Evening Mail

Monsieur G is not one of those discreet, faceless figures waiting behind bullet-proof glass off Bond Street for his prey and their sweethearts to drop in. He believes, like the itinerant Algerians who sell leather poofs in Paris restaurants, that his customers are at their most vulnerable when they have one hand round a brandy glass and the other on the knee of their investment.

The Sunday Times

City Tour £6 (£3) Daily departures. Duration 2 hours.
A drive through Geneva, where the quays and lakeside setting form a picturesque background to its landscaped parks, fountain and historic buildings. A visit to the International Centre which houses organisations such as UNO, WHO etc. is included.

Time Off brochure

Temporary leaners

ST LAWRENCE C.E. PRIMARY SCHOOL,
Cuckfield Road, Hurstpierpoint BN6 9SA.
Required 4th September 1984, generaly 10 hours per week

Brighton Evening Argus

THREE SISTERS (BBC-2, 10.20 p.m.) An earnest production of Russian author Chekov's great play centering on the boring lives of the song and dance. Dick Powell and Joan Blondell head the cast, which also features Ginger Rogers singing 'We're in the money'. One to lift your spirits and make you smile with nostalgia.

South Yorkshire Times

THE KAYDOR (Singles) Club invites unattacked people over 30 who enjoy dancing and are interested in music and theatre to join our social evenings every Tuesday at 8 p.m. in the Deanpark Hotel, Renfrew.

Glasgow Evening Times

Reviewing the current immigration rules, the briefing concedes that the much-criticised provision allowing non-U passport holders indefinite entry provided they have one British grandparent is ' undeniably anomalous."

The Grauniad

A BELFAST councillor last night claimed he had received a letter from the Northern Ireland Office which proved that the RUC Chief Constable, Sir John Hermon, had lied about the number of plastic pullets fired during the anti-internment rally in Andersonstown earlier this month at which Mr Sean Downes was killed.

Irish Times

CLERK OF WORKS

A full time experienced C.O.W. is required to supervise a £2.5m high quality housing development in Central Middlesbrough. The appointment is open from July/August and anticipated completion Jan/Feb 1985. Salary will be by negotiation.

Applications should be made in writing giving full details of qualifications and experience to:

Dixon Del Pozzo DHP (UK),
12 Huntingdon Street, St. Neots,
Cambridgeshire PE19 1BD

to be returned before June 30, 1983.

Durham Advertiser

Last year the society appointed Mr John Boyer. former deputy chairman of Hong Kong and Shanghai Bank, as its first chief expense.

Financial Times

LONDON, Dec. 8: Britain's Prince Andrew has a new girlfriend, the dark-haired, 21-year-old daughter of a film producer, a London newspaper reported today.
Victoria MacDonald is a danger and part-owner of a fashionable night club, the *Daily Express* said.

Kuwait Times

7.05—NATIONAL NEWS AND SPORT; Weather.
7.20—ZUBIN MEHTA MASTERCLASS. The work tackled tonight by the aspiring young conductors is one of the great works in the orchestral repertoire, Beethoven's "Erotica Symphony".

Jersey Evening Post

1952 Austin Sheerline Hearse body in resonable order, but engine not running, (head gasket). Garaged, £95,

Practical Classics

SEPARATED

Ins. Cooke said that following domestic trouble Mrs.
Keogh and her husband had
separated, and he had gone
to live with his sister. On
July 29 Mrs. Keogh went to
see him, and while they were
talking she pulled a small
potato from her handbag and
stabbed him. Fortunately the
injury was not as serious as
was at first thought.

Police sealed off the east-bound carriageway of the M4 at ewbury, Berkshire, for nine hours until 8 a.m. yesterday, while they rounded up 200 sheep which escaped from an overturned lorry.

Daily Telegraph

BANANA
OPENS
PARLIAMENT
See pages 2 – 4

Spotlight on Zimbabwe

PA

1 DIRECTORS Lunch

The humble packed lunch was transformed into a boxed banquet
today for Prince Charles and 4,000 top businessmen.

Inside the cardboard boxes distributed at the Institute of
Directors annual convention in London's Royal Albert Hall was a
veritable delight for the gourmet.

Nestling up to a plastic knife and fork were a mushroom hors
d'oeuvre, smoked children, syllabub and cheese - to be washed down
with wine, mineral water and 12-year-old malt whisky.

PA CORRECTION

DIRECTORS Lunch

In 1 DIRECTORS Lunch para three please read ''smoked chicken''.
NOT ''smoked children''. as sent.

end tsw

Press Association teleprint

LEWISHAM Leisure Centre is
about to launch a new set of
courses.

Each of the weekly courses — all
but one containing sex sessions —
begins at the centre in Rennell Street
in September.

Lewisham Outlook

'Thatcher's war chest is far bigger than anyone else's.

Toronto Globe and Mail

A wedding reception was held in Welton Village Hall, followed in the evening by a supper and dance. The bride and groom are enjoying their honeymoon in the Silage field.

Cumberland & Westmorland Herald

Iron Age boc

ARTHUR SCARGILL

LONDON (AP) — Part of the body of a red-bearded Iron Age man, preserved in a peat bog for 2,500 years, was displayed at the British Museum, revealing for the first time the face of a prehistoric Briton.

The corpse, found in a peat bog in central Britain in August, was briefly shown to reporters on Thursday.

Vancouver Sun

..DS Task Force: coloured prints by Robert Taylor. 'Sea King Rescue', Prince Andrew picks up survivors from Conveyor personally signed by Commander Wykes - Sneyd, size 27in. x 20in., £15. 'South Atlantic Task Force', ships featured 'Glamorgan', 'Ardent', Olna', 'Resource', Arrow', 'Herpes' and 'Sheffield', signed by Jeremy Moore, Commander Land Forces, size 20in. x 24in. Ellis, Castle Mill, Berry Pomeroy, Totnes.

Sunday Independent

Helen liked love making—jury told

HELEN SMITH "enjoyed making love," the inquest into her death heard today.

Tim Hayter, one of the last four people left at the party in Jeddah, Saudi Arabia, after which Helen died, siad: "There are many girls all over the world who enjoy ging to bed and making love.

"She was very honest about it also." .

His statements were mad.

Newcastle Evening Chronicle

The trustees of the Kedleston Estate went to the courts seeking guidance on their legal liabilities towards the beneficiaries of the estate of the second Lord Scarsdale, who died in 1977.

The beneficiaries were the present Lord Scarsdale and his five children, two of whom are miners.

The Times

At home

Baby and Coffee Grinder

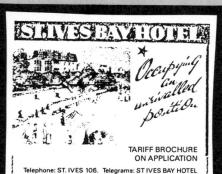

Other site owners are also standing out against the council's decision to issue compulsory purchase orders and a public inquiry will be held in Colchester on October 23 in a bed to resolve the issue.

Essex County Standard

**THE WORKERS' EDUCATIONAL
ASSOCIATION (Northern District)
BLYTH BRANCH, 1983-1984**

Birds in Northumberland (contd.)
Tutor: S. E. BIRD, L.D.S., M.B.O.U.
10 Meetings: Tuesd——

News. 5.05 **Blockbusters.**
5.35 **Robin Of Sherwood (T).** Start of a
new sex-part series based on the life
of the legendary folk hero, Robin Hood.

6.40 **The Fame Game.** 7.20 **All Star Secrets**

'BOROVERE', ALTON, HANTS. Luxury
hoe for retired gentlefolk in 2 acres. Close to
twon centre. Good food with every comfort.
BROCHURE. Tel. ————

Country Life

WIDOW cleaners required, on large
contract for Saturday work, experienced on ladders and with Squeegees.
— Tel. 01-504

Waltham Forest Extra

***

A PEDESTRIAN flasher will soon be erected outside Sea Point Boys' Junior School, High Level Road, Sea Point, if an Executive Committee recommendation is approved by the City Council.

The Cape Times

"I got up and White, who was in front of me, was going to head butt me. I had had no conversation with him until that moment," he told Maidstone Crown Court.

Mr Waller went on: "I hit him with a fish, which knocked him back, and bouncers threw him out."

South Kent Gazette

Small sties may solve gipsy problem

SMALL and scattered cara-van sites might be the

Hereford Times

Whipping boys

M. James, Cheltenham: "I'm surprised the stewards did not reprimand Christy Roche and Pat Eddery for excessive use of the ship during the Derby. It made me feel sick for the poor horses".

Daily Mirror

will be remembered by his many friends around the world for his enthusiasm in all he did, his strong personality and wise counsel.

He leaves a window.

The Times

WORKS MANAGER required for joinery division of large London based shoplifting company. Experience essential in managing a skilled workforce on short production runs and single units for high standards. An attractive package of salary and benefits will be available to the right applicant. Write W.M.12136, Daily Telegraph, E.C.4.

Daily Telegraph

ENGINEERS are mysti-
fied by a hole which
suddenly appeared in
Dawes Road, Fulham,
last week.

The hole caused traf-
fic to be diverted for
several hours.

A Council spokesman
said: "We don't know
what has caused this
hole, but the borough
engineers are looking
into it."

West London Observer

sure of a heartfelt vote of thanks from Hindus in the north-west.

Mrs Gandhi has often been accused of pandering to the Hindus to curry votes along communal lines.

The Times

With seven minutes gone the packed terraces erupted as Butler struck the ball into Liverpool's net but the linesman's fag was aloft indicating off-side.

The Observer

MAO'S WIDOW WILL NOT DIE

The Standard

Mujahideen seize two womens pies

The Pakistan Times

Prince Charles found himself ill prepared for the weather when he arrived at the Royal Showground in Stoneleigh today. However, within minutes he was supplied with flat tweed cap, umbrella and a crumpled weather proof jacket to fend off the driving rain at the British Fairy Farming Event.

Evening Mail

MATRIMONIAL AND FAMILY PROCEEDINGS BILL

On Wednesday, 13 June the Matrimonial and Family Proceedings Bill returned to the House of Commons from the special standing committee. After 5 hours of debate on that section of the bill which proposed shortening the time-limit from marriage to possible divorce down to 1 hour, the Solicitor-General, Sir Patrick Mayhew, rejected criticisms – many of them from his own party – that the Government was devaluing marriage. He told MPs that he was in favour of marriage as an institution and wished nothing to weaken it. He

Family Law

Dosbarthiadau Allanol Newydd
ABERYSTWYTH
New Extra-Mural Classes

TYMOR YR HAF

THE LIVING SEA
JOHN FISH, BSc, PhD

APOLOGY TO NEALES VIDEO

In last week's Bromsgrove Advertiser/Messenger we published an advertisement for Neales Video. A line of type from elsewhere reading "mounds of hardcore" inadvertently appeared on that advertisement.

We apologise to Neales Video for this error and should any of our readers have understood the advertisement as meaning that Neales Video deals or has dealt in obscene films we are happy to confirm that we accept that this is not so.

Bromsgrove Advertiser/Messenger

Office of the President
DEPARTMENT OF DEFENCE

TENDER NOTICE

TENDERS are invited for the manufacture/supply of the following items to the Armed Forces for the period ending June 30, 1985
DOD/411/1(319)83-85 — Supply of housewife basic complete.

The Kenya Times

ELIZABETHAN cassette recorder, as new. £11.50 —

Salcombe Gazette

Six Faces of Wine
CHALFONTS COUNTY SECONDARY SCHOOL
NICOL ROAD
Weds 7.45–9.15pm 6 fortnightly meetings 12 January 1983
Ms P Drinkwater

Buckinghamshire W.E.A. Brochure

Personal

I have placed before you an open door that no one can shut. Rev. 3 v.8.

A sauna and massage, Monday to Saturday. Tel. Ipswich

East Anglian Daily Times

About the author

For more than fifteen years, **Priscilla Elfrey** has specialized in helping managers and executives perform more effectively on the job. Currently Exec-

Mr Michael Guth, a senior licensing inspector said that when he visited the shop, which has a £95,000-a-year turnover, he found videos, audio tapes and books dealing mainly with flagellation and spanking.

Titles included Meek Mild and Obedient, Sexy College Girls Swimming Pool Spanking and Bottoms Up.

Mr Alan Cooper, for Janus, said his client had "bent over backwards" to comply with the council's regulations.

The Grauniad

CHICKEN DISHES

Moti Mahal Chicken	2 50
Muraghe Massla	2 30
Chicken Curry	1 70
Chicken Madras (F.Hot)	1 95
Chicken Vindaloo (V.Hot)	2
Chicken Bhuna	2

Long-range Outlook

Southern Ontario — Partly cloudy and cold tomorrow with scattered snotflurries near Lake Huron and Georgian Bay.

The Globe and Mail

12 10 - **12 35 HALL OF HORRORS** — Judaism. Professor James Mackay in conversation with Sir Immanuel Jacobovits ,chief rabbi of the United Hebrew Congregation of the British Commonwealth.
★★ Outstanding. · ★ Recommended.

Daily Telegraph

Quite a haul!

AMONG the haul taken from a house in Ashley Drive, Banstead, over the weekend were two fur goats, two diamond rings, gold cufflinks, a gold brooch and 140 Australian dollars.

Banstead Herald

Mrs Bingham, Therfield's headmistress, supported by staff, parents and "friends" kept everything· running smoothly at the starters' end while a retired headmaster now living in Barley presided at the finishing line.

There were obstacle courses, sack, skipping and running races; also egg and spoon although in the latter the eggs looked suspiciously like potatoes. Brave Mums acted as buggers as the children, oblivious of the heat, came hurtling down the course.

Royston Crow

The families do not need to speak French, but are asked to make the student fool at home and provide a separate room. The ideal family will contain at least two people,

Wigan Reporter

The storm was described as one of the worst spring onslaughts in memory to plague Massachusetts, triggering traffic accidents that included a 50-cat pile-up south of Boston.

Majorca Daily Bulletin

Mr Alf Parrish, Chief constable of Derbyshire, described suggestions that miners' telephones in the county had been tapped as nonsense.

The Times

Salisbury ban

FOUR people charged with trespass while following cruise missile convoys on Salibury Plain have been ordered to stray out of Wiltshire as part of bail conditions. Back page.

Grauniad

BUYING or SELLING a house could cost you dear. See a SOLICITOR... just to be SURE.

Yorkshire Evening Press

The magazine was started in 1955 on the premise that women wanted more from a magazine than knitting patterns and recipes and was the first to give space to frank discussions on topics such as sex, menstruation and cannibalism.

Marketing Week

ment yesterday. Also silent was the NSW branch of the Australian Funeral Directors' Association, a trade group representing about 140 funeral parlours around the State. Mr Ben Box, a member of the group's executive committee, said "the subject's been rehashed more times than I've had breakfast. We have nothing to say".

Sydney Morning Herald

At Blackfriars engineering Mr Hugh Marsh, the chairman, confirmed they had a break-in but not much of value was taken.

The thieves did a lot of damage, breaking into desks and ransacking offices there, but they only stole portable dictating machine and some jars of foreign coins, and Mr Marsh.

Redhill & Reigate News

HOSPITAL SMOKING BANNED

IN reply to a letter (January 29) I assure readers that Bristol General Hospital staff are not allowed to smoke on duty as we know how unpleasant and harmful this is for patients and their visitors.

Catherine Fagg
South Unit
Administrator
Bristol General
Hospital,

Bristol Evening Post

Look, snow clothes!

In Northumbria police say they have been plagued by complaints of children throwing snowballs. In one incident police answered an anonymous call after it was alleged that a man wearing dark sunglasses and a white pom pom hat was standing in the street exposing himself.

"We did indeed find somebody of that description — a snowman. He certainly didn't have any clothes on, but he wouldn't answer any questions. You could say he gave us the cold shoulder . . ." joked a police spokesman.

Dublin Evening Press

Belated birthday greetings
TO MY DARLING WIFE
Love you now and forever
JOHN AND NED

Bristol Journal

● **Mr Peter Tatchell being greeted by Miss Catherine Weare, chairman of Warwick and Leamington Young Socialists, on Tuesday outside the Oddfellows Hall in Leamington.**

Leamington Morning News

8.40 BBC Philharmonic Orchestra in Italy
leader DENNIS SIMONS
conductor EDWARD DOWNES
with JOAQUIN ACHUCARRO (piano)
Part 1
Bax Symphonic Poem: Tintagel
Ravel Piano Concerto in D for the left

Radio Times

Thursdays
Jan. to March 1985
1830 to 2030

The Best of British Geology?
A course for people with a background knowledge of geology including some sexperience in the field.

Geological Museum leaflet

A SALESMAN, an electrical supervisor, a businessman and the Vice-President of the Garda Representative Association will be fighting it out for the honour of being elected Kink of Dalkey.

Dublin Evening Press

THREE GIRLS, navy school skirts, age 11 years. £10 the lot. — Forton   (30c

Lancaster Grauniad

RAPE
A Public Demonstration of the
CALDWELL RAPE RANGER
Motorised Self-steering Bird Scarer
will be held at
Balspardon Farm, Gollanfield, Inverness
on Wednesday 13th February, 10 a.m.-3 p.m.
by kind permission of Mr J. Cattell

Aberdeen Press and Journal

BACHELOR Mervyn Stockwood, former Bishop of Southwark who has retired to Bath, will make history next month when he lays hands on a woman.

Bath and West Evening Chronicle

Margaret Thatcher was among many distinguished guests to Portland Place in festival year; president Michael Manser attends.

Building Design

DRAMA
Peter Freedman

Novelist Henry James was never much cop as a playwright during his lifetime. After his lifetime, although his output decreased, his theatrical success markedly increased with dramatisations of his novels penned by others.

Cosmopolitan

The Standard

Arresting sight

SUPER-SLIMMER PC Michael Sykes, from Bradford, Yorks, has gone from 16½ stone to 15 stone. He says: " The hardest thing is that every advert on TV seems to be for food.

" But my wife has joined me and that's helped. She's lost half a stone in a wee."

Sunday People

Pets

AFFECTIONATE 3 months old kitchen, needs kind home with garden. Stockton

Tees-side Times

FOR SALE BY AUCTION AT AN EARLY DATE UNLESS
PREVIOUSLY SOLD
OLD SPANKERS COTTAGE, 38 LIVERPOOL ROAD,
FORMBY
Rare opportunity: Unique Historic Thatched Cottage in poor state of repair, requiring complete refurbishment; large corner garden plot; hall, lounge, dining room, kitchen, 3 bedrooms, bathroom, sep. w.c.
All inquiries to the Formby Office

Formby Times

CND ducks call for hardline on Russia

Grauniad

Mr Kinnock said that Labour found the speculation against the pound both irresponsible and irrational, but they considered that the Government's handling " of the current crisis " s h o w e d " bumbling incompetence that is going to cost the industries and households of this country very dear."

The Prime Minister should " now help the pound by wacking the Chancellor of the Exchequer."

Daily Telegraph

Lord Lucan, a junior minister and the Government's only trade and industry spokesman in the House of Lords, was given a tour of the Centre for Advanced Technology.

Romsey Advertiser

ACCOUNTS CLERK

A knowledge of plumbing and central heating would be advantageous.

Applications in writing please, stating age and experience to The Managing Director, B. R. Biddle & Son Ltd., Lewis Lane, St Helier.

Jersey Evening Post

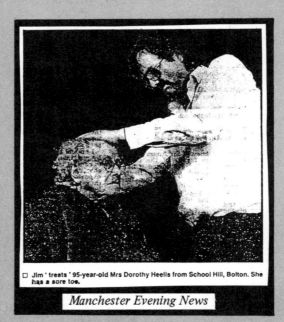

☐ Jim ' treats ' 95-year-old Mrs Dorothy Heells from School Hill, Bolton. She has a sore toe.

Manchester Evening News

Wild talk

THE Wandsworth branch fo the London Wildlife Trust has orgnised a talk on "Gardens for Wildlife." Mrs Robin Robbins will be speaking about London wildlife at the Northcote library in Battersea on April 18 at 7.30 pm . For further details phone 228 8228.

Streatham & Tooting News

'Crisis' call

EDUCATION SECRETARY Sir Keith Joseph was warned today that he must act to solve the crisis over pay and low morals, in the teaching profession, or he must go.

Liverpool Echo

'Big impact'

Mr Leslie Christie, assistant general secretary of the Society of Civil and Public Servants, which represents a majority of the 6,000 unformed Customs officers, predicted that the "big impact" of the protest action would come on Monday however.

Daily Telegraph

Ushiba Dies

Former External Economic Affairs Minister Nobuhiko Ushiba, a major figure in the rectum at Hanzomon Hospital in Tokyo's Chiyoda Ward at 7:40 a.m. Monday. He was 75.

After serving as vice foreign minister and ambassador to the United States, Ushiba

Ushiba

Asahi Evening News

NEXUS, we don't have space to tell you what we are so this is what we're not — A dating service or marriage bureau. If you're unattacked (any age) telephone the Scottish Office for a brochure. 041 221

Glasgow Herald

When Bingham announces his team at noon today he will almost certainly name either John McClelland or Sammy McIlroy as captain—a role McIlroy has undertak3n in the past, and that McClelland declined at club level with Watford a few months ago. There is less doubt that Pat Jennings will appear in gaol yet again.

Grauniad

Not only has the town's aging housing stock, including many derelict homes, been almost totally renovated but the town's sagging economy has been uplifted and more shops and firearms attracted to Wirksworth.

Daily Telegraph

After the mock trial, the spokesman said, she had been badly eaten and was admitted to the prison hospital with black eyes and a suspected broken jaw. On December 5, Helen was transferred to another prison.

Grauniad

A third-floor flat in Berkeley House, close to Berkeley Square, is offered by Beauchamp Estates at the recently reduced price of £260,000. It has three bedrooms and two reception rooms, with all the essential things for London living, including gold-plated electric switches and door handies.

Daily Telegraph

In many of the dozen cases, girls wept as they spoke of terrifying assaults in their homes, in the flats of "friends" or in open fields. Throughout the country other girls were undergoing similar ordeals in Crown Court witness boxes.

Daily Express

> Mr Williams, however, raises a valid point about too many fixtures. Cricket and football have suffered from the same disease and now rugby is displaying the same symptoms. The drain upon leading players grows; it is hard to imagine, for example, how New Zealand's leading players have coped with their respective employers during a winter whcih has brought a visist from France, a tour to Autralia and a tour to Fifi.

The Times